To Mol...

SOCIAL MEDIA ON AUTO

Grow Your Business and Revenue in Less Than 2 Hours A Month

Delicia Ivins

Good luck and reach out with any questions. You got this.
Delicia Ivins

Darling Jubilee Publishing

Social Media On Auto © 2023 by Delicia Ivins

Published by Darling Jubilee Publishing, Co.
Taylors, South Carolina 29687

Cover Illustration and Design: 100 Covers
Author Photo: Crystal Smith

All rights reserved. No part of this publication may be reproduced, distributed, or transmitted in any form or by any means, including photocopying, recording, or other electronic or mechanical methods, without the prior written permission of the publisher, except in the case of brief quotations embodied in critical reviews and certain other noncommercial uses permitted by copyright law.

Paperback ISBN 979-8-9875842-0-0
eBook ISBN 979-8-9875842-1-7

CONTENTS

Read This First	v
Foreword	ix
Introduction	xi
Note To The Reader	xix
1. Great Social Media Needs A Great Offer	1
2. Setting Up Your Social Media Lab For Success	11
3. Seeing The Opportunities In Front Of You—Overtaking The Competition Using Social Media	25
4. Creating your SEED Keyword and Hashtag Lists	37
5. Creating New Accounts & Optimizing Your Current Accounts To Rank on Google and Other Search Engines	53
6. Helping Others	67
7. How Much Content Do I Really Need?	73
8. What to write?	95
9. Understanding Reports and Analyzing Your Data	109
10. Goal Setting & Hiring Your Virtual Assistant	117
Bonus Chapter: Marketing for Business Growth 101	125
Acknowledgments	139
About the Author	141
Love this book?	143

READ THIS FIRST

To help speed up your Social Media on Auto results and get your accounts optimized, automated, and generating revenue faster than ever, I've created additional resources for you.

Get your copy of the Account Optimization Sheet, One-Page Overview, and more at:

SocialMediaOnAuto.Com/Resources

FREE RESOURCES

Resources and guides for people who want to
go fast,
get amazing results,
and do less work to get there.

SOCIAL MEDIA ON AUTO
...FAST PASS...

I would like to dedicate this book to my husband and best friend, Ben, as well as to my amazingly creative daughters, Caroline and Bonnie, and to my clients.

Truly, writing this book turned out to be a bigger commitment than I originally projected. I am wildly blessed to have you all as my partners in adventure on this turn around the globe.

Ben, thank you for letting me play in your medium. You gave the team and me such great and engaging content to work with that it made planning and scheduling social media fun.

To my girls:
I adore you both more than you could even begin to comprehend. This is your playground, a vision for you and your generation to realize. Enjoy the process, have fun, and above all else, be love in motion.

To my clients:
Thank you for allowing my team and me to serve you. We have enjoyed working with you all and helping your businesses grow.

FOREWORD

I'm excited to write this introduction for *Social Media on Auto*. As someone who has helped businesses optimize their social media channels, I know firsthand the challenges that come with cutting through the noise and reaching the right people.

In my bestselling book, co-authored with Perry Marshall, *The Definitive Guide to TikTok Advertising*, I walk readers through the process of optimizing a single, focused channel, TikTok, for increased traffic and revenue, reaching millions of people, through ad set-up and management.

In *Social Media on Auto*, Delicia takes a different path. This book breaks down the exact systems she uses to help local businesses automate their entire social media presence and create a powerful brand following that drives revenue and sales by reaching the exact people who are going to spend money with you—people in your community.

This book is like having an expert personal social media assistant at your fingertips. Sit back, relax, and let the book guide you through the process of optimizing your social channels to reach and convert more people in your local area using reusable content so you don't have to invent 60+ pieces of new content every month.

Delicia's step-by-step processes are well thought-out, intentional, and cost- and time-effective. She breaks down the complicated world of social media into easy-to-follow steps that anyone can implement. Using "Build Your Business" exercises in each chapter, Delicia walks you through step-by-step processes to build a social media machine that, once built, you can hand over to someone else to pull the levers for you, freeing up your time immensely.

As someone who values systemization and minimizing downtime on ineffective strategies, I'm a big believer in optimization through simplification. As she mentions in the book, by following the 80/20 Principle, you can minimize the time and effort you put into managing your social media channels and still see great results.

Dennis Yu

Las Vegas, NV

Dennis's newest book, co-authored with Perry Marshall, The Definitive Guide to TikTok Advertising, is available to purchase at any major bookstore or book retailer. In an explosive release, the book teaches readers how to reach one billion people in ten minutes.

INTRODUCTION

"Yeah, I'm just so booked, man." "I don't know whether to hire a second shooter or to block off more time for myself."

I eavesdropped, listening in to my husband chatting with his brother about how slammed his calendar was for the next few weeks.

He continued, "Last year, I would wake up and be booked maybe one or two days out." "This year, I'm booking weeks out in advance."

The real estate industry is hot where we live right now. And Ben, with his solid work ethic, attention to detail, creative composition and use of light, and an eye for opportunity, well, he's in high demand.

People tell him all the time, "It's a good problem to have."

He's had shoots for 10-million-dollar mansions. This year, his work was featured in *atHome Magazine*, a South Carolina magazine for luxury living. You would think, with this much business, we would be pouring money into ads, spending hours

INTRODUCTION

promoting him in social media, and doing tons of networking events.

Ben is only three years into his business. His first job was forty-five minutes away. He showed up with a simple Canon camera and only made $75. He's grown 40% year over year for the last two years.

But why am I telling you about my husband's real estate photography business? Why does it matter? This book is supposed to be about social media marketing.

It started as most stories do these days: during COVID. We had recently returned from a one-year sabbatical we took with our family—a one-year trip around the US, touring national parks with our kids in an RV. When we returned to our home state of South Carolina, we decided to stay awhile. We parked the RV, took up residence in a small, 950-square-foot home we had been renting out while we were on the road, and began to assess what we wanted to do with our lives.

Ben had spent the last ten years as a bicycle mechanic. He loved the culture but not the pay. It wasn't enough to provide for our family. I had spent the last eight years working part-time as a marketing manager for a small, locally owned pet nutrition store and learning about digital marketing.

With little budget to work with, my goal at my marketing job was to make every dollar ROI-positive for this mom-and-pop shop. I started learning about online marketing and the power of blogging and social media for businesses in 2008. As the pet events dwindled in attendance, I had to look for other ways to bring in new clients and revenue, forcing me to get very creative. I learned on-the-fly, testing new marketing techniques and purchasing online courses to teach me what colleges weren't yet teaching.

INTRODUCTION

Fast forward back to 2018, and we were in our little house. As I unpacked our 350-square-foot RV into our 950-square-foot home, I found myself flipping through photos Ben had taken of our kids. To say they were amazing would be an understatement. Using the exact same smartphone as me that year, his photos captured emotion, movement, and light way better than any "mom with her phone" snapshots I had taken that year.

I asked myself, "He's so good." "How can he make money with this?" I picked up my phone off the floor where I was sitting and looked up our neighborhood's listings on Zillow and Redfin, taking note of the pictures of for-sale homes that realtors had taken with their phones. There were homes listed at $250,000 and up, with a realtor's reflection in the mirror and patchy grass in the yard. I brought my phone in and sat down by Ben on the couch.

"Look at this. I mean, look. This is terrible. You can do this. You could do real estate photography and kill it." We purchased a $500 Canon camera on Amazon that night and set out to get Ben clients using LinkedIn, Canva flyers, and no website.

Ben grew pretty quickly that first year. By year two, I decided to leave the position I was in, working as a project manager for people who wanted to build online courses and sales funnels for their businesses. At-home learning during COVID was taking a lot of my attention, and my kids needed me. During the break, I asked Ben what I could do to alleviate some pressure for him. I couldn't shoot; I didn't have his eye, but I had nine years of marketing experience, so maybe I could help there.

I looked through his social media and began to optimize each channel for search engine traffic and conversions, and I got traffic coming through his social media to convert into leads or customers for his business. Little things, like optimizing his

INTRODUCTION

Google My Business profile, got him in the Google 3-Pack literally overnight. (The Google 3-Pack consists of the top three Google Maps listings on a local business search.) I was sending the right signals, and the internet liked them. Ben's social media profiles and Google My Business listing now showed on page one of Google for search terms like "real estate photographer Greenville, SC."

I asked myself how I could make the signal to Google stronger for those looking for a real estate photographer in our area. I started playing with Google ads. We weren't spending a ton—less than $300 a month—but Google noticed.

During this time, Ben was creating all his own posts and content. Trying to stay relevant and post one to two times a week was a lot on top of his already busy schedule, but I knew that posting at least once a day was what it would take to take over the social scene for real estate photographers in our area.

I also knew I couldn't ask him to do that. He was already running at full speed, all gas, no brakes. I didn't have the time to fully commit to running and managing his social media myself, nor did I want to. I had two kids in a mix of virtual school and homeschool, and I had decided to get back in the saddle and take on client work, working with smaller clients at a slower pace so that I could prioritize my family. I also knew from first-hand experience that social media, with the wrong strategy, could become a time suck with little to no return. Time is not a commodity I give up easily.

So I did what I like to do in situations like this. I created a strategy. I analyzed what his competitors were doing and crossed that information with what top names in the industry were doing in the US. I joined a coaching program. I took a few courses. Then, I created a 98% hands-off strategy to manage his social media.

INTRODUCTION

The strategy I use for my clients and what I will teach you in this book is 98% evergreen. I don't chase social media trends—no TikTok dances or challenges here. It also takes less than two hours per month if you use the systems I show you, including using a virtual assistant to help create content. And, to make it even better, I'll teach you how to pull it together with a little SEO magic to use your social media accounts to help you rank on page one on search engines like Google—just like I do for my clients.

Ben still posts to social media occasionally now, mostly for fun. He doesn't worry about hashtags, reach, or engagement because he knows we have those in the bag. He now has the luxury of only posting when he feels inspired. Because his social media accounts are updated daily, he stays top of mind with all his existing realtors and gains new clients often.

I've overheard new clients ask Ben on an initial phone call, "If I hire you, will you share these house photos on your social profiles?" because they know that Ben's profile will get their listings more exposure. They're not just paying for real estate photography. They're paying for real estate photography and marketing—a chance to be featured on his page. So, Ben can charge higher prices than many in the market.

As we stay on top of his Google My Business listing, he stays in the top Google 3-pack search for real estate photographers. Today, he had three calls in less than two hours from people he's never worked with looking to book him on a shoot.

Ben now focuses on what he loves to do: shoot houses and have fun. And let's be real—there's still stuff he doesn't love to do—but he's now able to process and systemize those things as well. Because he doesn't have to stress about creating content or trying to stay top of mind with clients, he gets to test new fun social media tricks regularly—like shooting video of one of his realtor clients falling into a pool for IG Reels and TikTok. He gets to play.

Social Media On Auto is not a "30 days to fully booked" promise.

But it is a promise.

> It is a promise of getting your time back...
>
> It is a promise of staying top of mind for your clients to increase and maintain client retention...
>
> It is a promise to reduce your stress...
>
> It is a promise of finding social media for your business fun again...

And if you follow the strategies I outline in this book, it is a promise of continued growth, year over year, for less than two hours a month of your time.

After spending thirteen years in online marketing, working on everything from websites to ads to traffic and social media to increase brand recognition to conversion funnels, I know one thing really well: systems make the world go round. Once you have solid systems in place, you can take your hand off stirring that pot and turn your attention to other revenue-generating (or even relaxation) activities.

The strategies and systems I will teach you in this book are designed to be implemented in as little as one week, but could take you up to thirty days, depending on your dedication to this project and your commitment to getting your time back.

Once up and running, you'll see your social media post reach and engagement tick up between 20% and 200%, depending on

INTRODUCTION

how well you follow what I'll teach you. Our first month, we saw more than 40% growth, and that was when I was just starting out.

In this 30-day sprint to automate your social media, I'll teach you how to think strategically. I'll show you how to see the patterns and how to read the algorithm matrix. It's up to you to apply the strategy and do the work.

I will go ahead and tell you that the key to getting this system running like a machine will be hiring a reliable virtual assistant for your business to handle your posts for you. But don't worry about that right now; I'll teach you how to do that as well.

Social media, done right, can fulfill all the promises I mentioned earlier without having you do crazy TikTok dances or Ice Bucket Challenges. It can position you as an authority in your sphere and grow your business and your influence in the community. It can level you up and get you access to clients and the lifestyle you desire.

You may read this and think, "Thirty days?" "I don't have that time right now." I encourage you to make the time. Once you build the system, you'll have an automated system that will help you build your brand this year, the year after that, and for years to come.

You've probably heard it before. "The best time to buy a house was ten years ago." "The next best time to buy a house is today." The longer you wait to get started, the longer you'll wait to have your time back while growing your business on autopilot.

And, if one day you decide that real estate photography is no longer for you, well, you could sell your successful business, fully branded, for a great price and add that to your retirement fund or take a very nice year-long trip yourself.

INTRODUCTION

But what if you're reading this as a realtor? You can roll your brand over to a winning agency or start your own brokerage.

It's time to dive in. In Chapter 1, "How Marketing Works," I'm going to teach you how to build an effective social media funnel to grow your brand, grow your traffic, and bring in leads. Let's get started.

NOTE TO THE READER

Everyone who picks up this book has a different level of understanding of what's involved in social media marketing, sales funnel building, customer journey mapping, and creating offers.

This book is written to help readers move quickly through implementation. As such, Chapter 1 starts with reviewing your offers to make sure they line up with your content and create a seamless journey for your customers.

If the terms I just used seem foreign to you, don't stop reading. I wrote this book for you, too. After Chapter 10, you'll find a bonus chapter titled "Marketing for Business Growth 101."

In the bonus chapter, I break down marketing ideas that I build on throughout the book. I also give a glossary of common social media and internet marketing terms so that you can understand and use the strategy in this book to become the local expert in your area. You'll also be able to dazzle your friends and colleagues with your newfound expertise in marketing jargon.

If you feel that an overview of marketing terms and concepts would be helpful for you before you jump into the material, begin by reading the Bonus Chapter at the end of this book first, then come back to Chapter 1 to get started.

It's important for me to tell you that I see you—hustling day in and day out. You can do this. I believe in you.

Here's to your journey,

Delicia

P.S. This book was written based on the work that I have done with my clients. As such, I use real estate agents and real estate photography business owners as examples throughout the book. However, if you are a small business owner with a service-based business, <u>this book will work for you</u>. Simply adjust the examples and stories to fit your industry.

ONE
GREAT SOCIAL MEDIA NEEDS A GREAT OFFER

Time spent creating and testing new offers is what I call a $10,000/hour activity. If you want to grow and scale your business, that's where you need to focus your energy.

I'm including this section before we get into breaking down social media because your content will directly speak to your offers. The better the offer, the better your content will perform to help you gain new clients and stay top-of-mind for the ones you have.

THE FUNNEL FRAMEWORK

What is a marketing funnel?

A marketing funnel is a visual way to show a potential customer's journey from "problem awareness" to buying your product or service (and hopefully being so happy with the experience that they come back to you again).

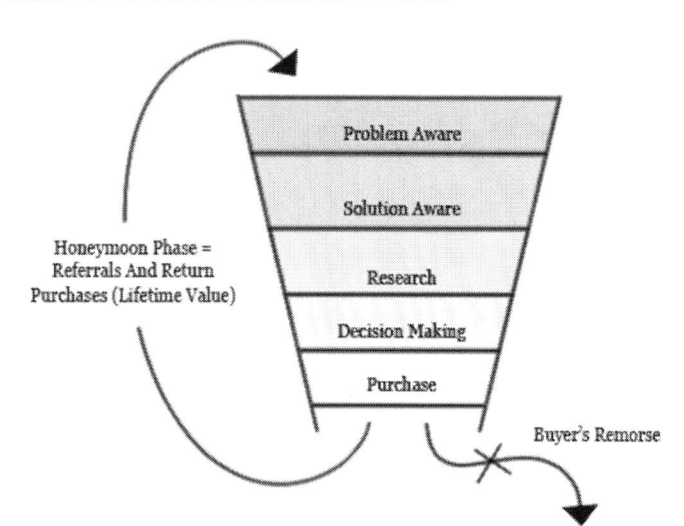

THE FUNNEL FRAMEWORK

```
                    Problem Aware
                    Solution Aware
Honeymoon Phase =
Referrals And Return   Research
Purchases (Lifetime Value)
                    Decision Making
                    Purchase
                              Buyer's Remorse
```

How Can You Apply This to Your Business?

Every day, your prospective customers are making decisions. In marketing, we commonly use the "funnel framework" to simplify and break down the process of how decisions are made in the customer journey.

In this breakdown, all decisions—any decision requirement—from small commitments, like where to go for coffee, to large commitments, like which house to buy, are made using the same foundational steps.

A Customer Journey Story

Sally decides that, as a new realtor on the scene, she needs new business—and fast. She spends two weeks researching—from online articles to courses to asking her mentor and other successful realtors to listening to podcasts. She decides the simplest, fastest way to get new clients is to ask her network for referrals, attend live networking events, and begin online organic marketing to help build know, like, and trust.

She quickly realizes that she needs to stand out in the flooded marketplace and build a brand for herself to differentiate herself. She sees a post by a headshot photographer for "fun, niche-style branded headshots." As a soccer mom herself, she decides to test marketing herself as the "Soccer Mom Realtor," working with sports families in her area on busy schedules, attending events, getting photo ops, and handing out cards. She decides to get a headshot for her social media profiles—a photo of her balancing a soccer ball on top of her head.

01 Problem Aware:

Sally needs new business.

02 Solution Aware:

Sally decides to market herself.

03 Research:

Sally researches for two weeks. She reviews all options presented: online ads, print ads, a blow-up gorilla, joining Toastmasters, attending network events, advertising on a billboard, using social media, etc.

04 Decision Making

Sally reviews the qualitative and quantitative data. How well did each of these campaigns work for the person who tried them? How much time was needed from them? What was the return on their investment? Sally decides on three components to grow her business: utilize her network, attend events and grow her network, and build her online brand.

05 Purchase:

Sally remembers the post she saw a couple of weeks ago and visits the social media profile of the headshot photographer. She reviews the fun headshot photos on the profile page and makes a decision to have headshots done of her with the soccer ball, and she places that photo on her Instagram, Facebook, and LinkedIn profiles.

06 Honeymoon Phase or Buyer's Remorse:

After 45 days of posting sports photos at local events and of handing out business cards at youth sporting events when volunteering, Sally has received fifteen calls and has three deals in her pipeline. Sally is in the honeymoon phase. She decides to continue this branding strategy, pulling it into her website copy, and commits to a full branded photoshoot with the photographer.

⇨ BUILD YOUR BUSINESS EXERCISE: YOUR IDEAL CLIENT

I want you to take some time to think about and describe your ideal client.

Get a blank sheet of paper and a pen. Set a timer for ten minutes. List the characteristics and traits of your ideal client.

Who do you want to work with and for?

> TIP: If you're already in business, think of your favorite customers, which are often the same ones that drive 20% of your business revenue.

What do you love about working with them?

List as many characteristics as you can think of in ten minutes.

MAPPING YOUR SERVICE ARC

When you use the information from your funnel or decision-making framework to create the path to your ideal customer's happiness, you both win. Mapping your service arc is a way to think through this process.

In the next two exercises, you will create a list of problems your ideal clients have and then list creative solutions that your business can offer to solve these problems for them. Make sure to do these exercises separately and in order. We'll reuse the work you're doing here later in the book, so it's best to save your work on your computer or in a notebook set aside for this book.

⇨BUILD YOUR BUSINESS EXERCISE: THEY GOT FIFTY PROBLEMS

Your ideal client or customer has fifty or more problems, but you shouldn't be one of them. In this exercise, make a list of fifty problems your ideal client has, along with solutions that you or your business offers.

⇨BUILD YOUR BUSINESS EXERCISE: MAPPING YOUR SERVICE ARC

Review the fifty problems you listed. Number them in order of importance to your ideal client.

Number one solves the biggest need—the biggest pain point—for your client. If their number one problem is building their brand, how can you help them solve it? If the number one problem you hear is finding stagers for the house, how can you help them solve this?

Problem number two should be the second-largest pain point they have, and so on.

Next, answer the questions below for the top three problems on your list. At the end, you'll have three Service Arcs mapped out for the three most common problems that your ideal clients face.

> TIP: Try to forget about what your current offers are for now and open yourself to creative solutions to these questions. Write your answers down on a sheet of paper.

1. If I could wave a magic wand and instantly deliver the best results for my clients, what would that process look like? For me? List every step you can think of.
2. What things could I take off their plate that my business does exceedingly well?
3. How would that make them feel?
4. What would need to be included so that I could deliver on this offer? Do they need a shared Google Drive folder to review all the photos? Do they need someone to write the copy for them?
5. How can my client set me up to deliver the best product or service?
6. What should I charge (based on the value I am delivering)?

After you've written your answers for solutions to problems one, two, and three, I want you to map your service arc.

Mapping your ideal customer's service arc will allow you to shift your perspective and see new opportunities to grow and scale your business. This allows you to broaden your horizons and come up with new offers to meet your clients where they are—in their time of need.

This also serves as a terrific basis for a type of content I'll show you later called "problem/solution" posts.

As we move into crafting your social media content in the following chapters, knowing your offers and common problems or objections in the marketplace is key. Social media is a great place to try out new deals and come up with creative ideas. It also gives you a place to promote new services at higher prices.

Below, I've included a sample service arc for a headshot photographer. All pricing and offer ideas are ones that I have made up for this example but could be tested in the marketplace.

SERVICE ARC EXAMPLE

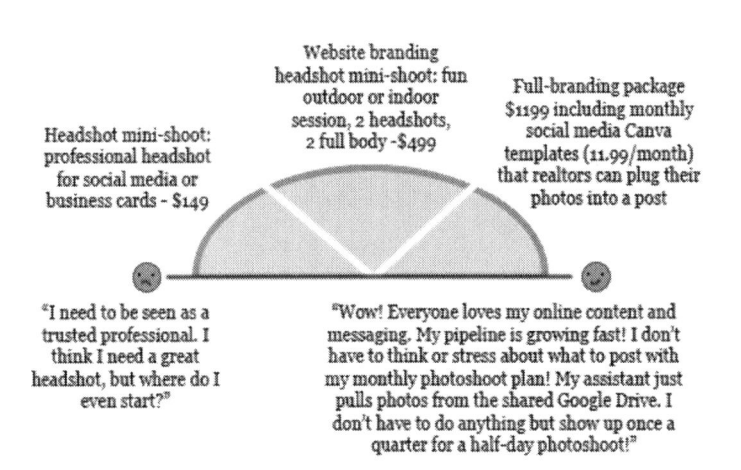

Headshot mini-shoot: professional headshot for social media or business cards - $149

Website branding headshot mini-shoot: fun outdoor or indoor session, 2 headshots, 2 full body - $499

Full-branding package $1199 including monthly social media Canva templates ($11.99/month) that realtors can plug their photos into a post

"I need to be seen as a trusted professional. I think I need a great headshot, but where do I even start?"

"Wow! Everyone loves my online content and messaging. My pipeline is growing fast! I don't have to think or stress about what to post with my monthly photoshoot plan! My assistant just pulls photos from the shared Google Drive. I don't have to do anything but show up once a quarter for a half-day photoshoot!"

MINDSET AND SETTING EXPECTATIONS

Before we move on to setting up your systems, it's important to do a quick mindset check.

Remember: marketing is a science. It follows the scientific method we all learned in elementary school.

THE SCIENTIFIC METHOD

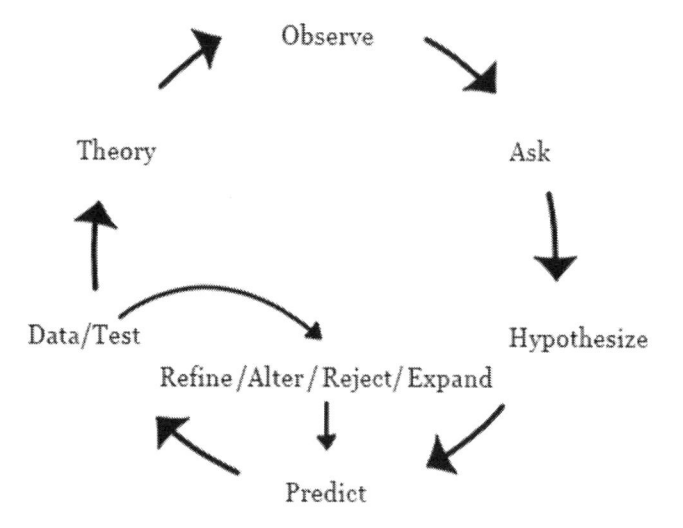

```
          Observe
   Theory         Ask
                    ↓
Data/Test       Hypothesize
      Refine/Alter/Reject/Expand
           Predict
```

In the following chapters, I'll break down my simple content creation strategy and process and give you templates and tricks I've learned from my thirteen years of online marketing experience.

What you need to remember is this: "Every day is an experiment."

If you approach the rest of this book with the same curious and joyful disposition you had at age six, creating potions of sticks, dirt, and flowers in your backyard, this entire experience will be a lot of fun. I promise.

And, at the end of it all, you'll have a system you can turn over to someone else to manage for you, if you so choose, reducing your total time commitment to two hours a month.

What are you going to do in those two hours? All you'll have to do is review reports and set goals for your virtual assistant for the next month.

That's it. Are you ready?

FOCUS POINTS

At the end of each chapter, I'll offer a quick recap of the main points covered in "Focus Points."

Focus points are the main points you need to know and remember for this automation journey to be successful for you.

In this chapter, we covered:

- A breakdown of the customer journey via an overview of the marketing funnel.
- How to shift how you think about marketing using the Scientific Method as you move into goal setting.
- ⇒Build Your Business Exercise: Your Ideal Client
- ⇒Build Your Business Exercise: They Got 50 Problems
- ⇒Build Your Business Exercise: Mapping Your Service Arc

Please make sure you complete the exercises before moving on to the next chapter.

TWO
SETTING UP YOUR SOCIAL MEDIA LAB FOR SUCCESS

WHERE DOES SOCIAL MEDIA FIT IN?

Using Social Media Effectively

There are three main traffic-driving channels in online marketing. They are organic (free traffic), paid (paid traffic to your website from ads), and affiliate traffic (traffic from other people and businesses you partner with). Social media is a subchannel of organic marketing.

Social media functions best as a top-of-funnel channel, targeting people at the "unaware" or "problem-aware" stages to bring in traffic and then leading them to the main business website.

It can also be used to post and show middle-of-funnel content. This is content that answers questions that come up during the solution awareness, research, and decision-making phases. However, ideally, 80% of the content you post on social media should do two main things: get people's attention and turn that attention into leads, usually by sending them to your website.

But what are the "right" and "wrong" ways to grow an account? How does an account get flagged or listed as tainted? It's easier than you think, and most people simply don't know better. I mean, how many people actually read the Terms of Use when they sign up for a social media account today? Fewer than you think.

People get direct messages or hear of people who have grown their account rapidly using so-and-so service, where one minute, they had twenty followers, and a couple of hundred bucks later, they had five hundred followers.

People like to find cheat codes. They want faster, quicker ways of achieving the same result. If you're reading this and you're old enough to remember the Game Genie for the original Nintendo, you understand exactly what I'm talking about here.

So here is a quick list of why this strategy doesn't really serve you long term:

#1: **Bought followers are sometimes spam followers.**

Do you ever see someone's feed or read through the comments on their social media posts, and it looks like random spam people trying to talk about their service, business, or cross-post their links? Yep. That's a risk you run. Additionally, a lot of your bought followers may not be in your target audience.

#2: **Many bought followers are just that—bought for a price to click a link and "follow" you.**

After that, the attention stops. They don't like, comment, or share your posts. So you have a large number of followers but no engagement, giving you a very low engagement score.

Social media accounts get flagged by the social media algorithms as "uninteresting" due to a low engagement score regularly. When engagement is low, the algorithm will stop showing your posts in the feed, even to your true followers and fans. Having little to no engagement on your accounts penalizes you. It's better to have real followers who are engaged with your content, and a higher engagement score.

Remember: Social Media platforms make money by showing ads. The longer people stay on their platforms, the more ads they get to show. So the more engaging your content, the more people look at it, like it, stay on the platform, the more ads they can show.

#3: Instagram (and probably others) purges fake accounts pretty regularly.

Instagram gets it—they want people to have a good experience, so they make regular rounds of fake account purges from their system. So those followers you bought—may disappear.

#4: Buying fake followers is against the Terms of Service.

For Instagram or Facebook, buying followers is a no-no. Facebook will allow you to buy "page likes" legally, but you can still wind up with low or no engagement, or audiences that don't match your dream customer. Meaning all the content you are creating will fall on deaf ears.

Now, for a little tough love.

If you have used any of the strategies above to grow your account, I recommend creating new accounts that you will use with the strategy presented in this book. As Instagram coach Eddie Smith said, "It's better, easier, faster, and you'll get more engagement just by starting a new account and growing it the right way."

Instagram and Facebook have likely already flagged your account for breaking the rules, and if they haven't shut you down, they're just not interested in showing your content. Look at this as a great opportunity to update your branding and look. But don't go creating new accounts just yet.

In chapters two through four, I'll teach you what to look for and how to set up your current (or new) social media accounts correctly. Then, in chapter five, you will do an exercise to make any new accounts you need based on the research you did in chapters two through four.

Still not sure if you need to create new accounts? Use the "Build Your Business Exercise: Social Media Account Audit" provided to help you get clarity.

⇨BUILD YOUR BUSINESS EXERCISE: SOCIAL MEDIA ACCOUNT AUDIT

Answer these quick questions to determine if you need to build new social media accounts or simply optimize your existing ones.

- Have you ever tried a follow/unfollow tactic on any of your social media channels in order to grow accounts?

Follow/unfollow is a common strategy often seen in groups or threads. In a follow/unfollow strategy, a group of people will agree to follow one another on a platform of choice, to boost the follow numbers quickly. This is problematic because it can cause your followers to be inflated with people who aren't the ideal customer for your business, increasing the chances of a low engagement score (people who aren't really fans of your content, just followed you so you would follow them back), as well as cause temporary "pops" or boosts in your followers in a single day or over a couple of days—which can trigger the algorithm to look at your account.

If you have tried follow/unfollow with any of your accounts—make a list of them.

- **Have you ever "bought" followers?**

If "yes", which accounts did you buy followers for?

- **Have you ever used "bots" to grow your account?**

Whether you coded it yourself, or hired someone to code it for you, using bots is dangerous. Once the social media platform detects a bot on your account, your account will be banned.

If you answered "yes" to any of the questions above, you need to build new accounts to replace the tainted ones.

I'll show you how to set up your new accounts correctly in Chapter 5. Before you go there, you must know which account types you need, how to overtake your competition, how to rank for key terms on search engines, and so much more. This information is covered in this chapter, Chapter 3, and Chapter 4.

⇨ BUILD YOUR BUSINESS EXERCISE: CALCULATE YOUR ENGAGEMENT SCORE

For any accounts that you have grown purely organically, the next step is to understand how well the accounts are performing in and of themselves.

Using the engagement score equation below or your social media scheduling tool (if you are using one that includes an analytics dashboard), calculate your engagement score for each platform you currently post on for the last 30 days of content.

Engagement Score Equation:

> For Instagram, for example, the engagement score is calculated by taking the total engagement (likes, comments, shares, views, etc.) and dividing it by the total number of followers.
>
> So, if your post had 15 comments and 5 shares and you had 500 followers, your engagement score for that post would be calculated as follows:
>
> 15 + 5 = 20
>
> 20/500 = 0.04 x 100 = 4% Engagement Score

To make things easier for you, I created a tool to help guide you through each step of the account optimization process as we continue—the Account Optimization Sheet.

To access your Account Optimization Sheet, go to SocialMediaOnAuto.com/Resources. Save a copy of the spreadsheet to your device to enable editing access.

When you have found or calculated your engagement score on Facebook, LinkedIn, and Instagram, log your score in the engagement score columns provided inside the spreadsheet on the Account Prep tab.

After you complete the strategy in this book and your social media accounts are automated and humming along, I recommend checking and comparing engagement score metrics on each platform monthly as part of your two-hour check-in process per month.

PERSONAL ACCOUNTS VERSUS BUSINESS ACCOUNTS

Each social media channel performs best with its own strategy specifically tailored to that platform. In other words, Facebook does best when you create a strategy that Facebook wants to show in its algorithm. This means that posting the same exact content everywhere isn't going to give you the best results. However, with these companies updating their algorithms daily, what normal person can stay on top of that?

Social media does a great job keeping your brand name top-of-mind with consumers and clients and has the capacity to give your brand amazing top-of-funnel reach (without spending money on ads.) It's definitely worth trying to be all places at all times—IF we can simplify the strategy.

If you're looking to create new accounts, you'll want to read the next section carefully to make sure that you create the right accounts for your business model.

Personal social media accounts can serve as well or better than business accounts for some businesses; it just depends on your long-term objectives and what you want out of each social media platform or channel (Facebook versus LinkedIn, for example).

Note: You won't be creating social media accounts just yet. We'll get into that in chapter five. In this chapter, you'll learn the pros and cons of personal and business accounts so that you can make sure that when you build your new accounts later, you're optimizing for the right strategy.

ACCOUNTS YOU NEED TO GET STARTED

Depending on your current business model, you will need a mix of personal and business social media accounts.

Subcontractors, Freelancers, Or Real Estate Agents

Personal Accounts

If you are a subcontractor, freelancer, or real estate agent, for now, you need personal accounts for the following social media channels:

- LinkedIn
- YouTube
- Facebook

Why?

LinkedIn personal accounts get more interactions and page views than business accounts at the moment. Since our strategy is based on getting effective channels set up and automated in thirty days or less, I don't want you to get distracted with creating or managing accounts that won't return the results you're looking for.

Effective YouTube marketing is a separate strategy—really, a separate book. In this book, I'll only be focusing on basic search engine optimization for YouTube videos and utilizing

YouTube as a storage library or portfolio to showcase any work you have done.

If you're a business owner that creates or uses a lot of video content naturally as part of your current process and you don't already have a YouTube channel account, you'll want to set one up. If you don't create or have access to a lot of video content in your existing business marketing assets, you can skip this for now.

With Facebook, a personal profile is required to set up your Facebook Page and Instagram business profile. Make sure you have a personal Facebook account so that you can set up your business accounts in the next step.

Business Accounts

You need the personal accounts to set up the business accounts. Why business accounts?

Business accounts give you added bonuses and added control. Business accounts allow access to analytics, user data, and the ability to add someone (later) as your social media manager to your account. Additionally, some social media scheduling software (that I'll discuss later in the book) only works with business accounts.

You will need business pages or accounts for:

- Facebook
- Instagram
- Google My Business

The goal is to optimize set-up on the channels to give you the most reach, eliminating extra steps that can be distracting at this stage.

While it's not a social media channel, if you don't have a Google My Business listing set up for your business yet, you'll want to create that account as well. You'll be using a Google My Business page in addition to social media to drive traffic and create revenue for your business. (And yes, this can be automated as well.)

Real Estate Photography Business Owners, Real Estate Brokerage, Any Company with Employees or Subcontractors

Personal Accounts

For existing businesses (three years old or more), if the CEO or business owner does not have their personal social media accounts established for LinkedIn, YouTube, and Facebook, I recommend doing that now so that you can create your business pages for these accounts next.

For example, if you have a real estate agency company named "Best Real Estate Agency," first, make sure that Jane Best has personal profiles set up for LinkedIn, Facebook, and Instagram. Then, set up business pages for LinkedIn, Facebook, Instagram, YouTube, and Google My Business under the business name, in this case, "Best Real Estate Agency."

> *Note: If Jane does not have these personal profiles (Instagram, Facebook, and YouTube) set up first, the company will be unable to set up the business pages required to move forward.

While an employee could set up the business pages for the business under their own personal account, this is a bad idea, as employees come and go. This can leave the business in a state of flux and stranded later when trying to regain control of social media accounts set up by a previous employee or contractor that they are no longer in touch with.

*Note: If Jane has a personal Instagram profile that she (1) uses a lot or mainly for business and (2) has a good amount of followers on, she can convert that personal profile into an Instagram business account.

MIGRATING AN EXISTING PERSONAL ACCOUNT INTO A BUSINESS ACCOUNT

Instagram has an option that allows you to change your personal Instagram account over to a business account—but this should only be done if your personal account could also work for your business. Before you do this, think: do my past personal posts generate know, like, and trust for my business and encourage people to contact me or get to know more about me, or did I just post pictures of my kids, coffee, and my dog for the last ten months? If 80% or more of the posts on your Instagram account are about your business, convert that personal Instagram profile into a business account. If, however, more than 20% of your posts on your Instagram account are personal in nature, I recommend creating a new Instagram account for your business.

If you intend to test ads at some point, you also want to set up business pages for Facebook and Instagram, as ads can *only be run on business pages*. Business pages on Facebook and Instagram also give you access to their advanced analytics for business pages dashboards—trust me—you'll want this later.

Business Accounts

If you own a business, brokerage, or any type of company with employees or subcontractors, you'll need business accounts set up for LinkedIn, Facebook, Instagram, YouTube, and a Google My Business Page.

The difference being, where an agent or contractor can use a personal account for LinkedIn and YouTube (for personal branding), for an established business, you'll want to take the extra step to make sure all your accounts are branded with your business name.

To allow someone to manage your social media in the future for you (i.e., schedule posts for you), you have to have business pages set up for Facebook and Instagram.

> **Remember, your goal is to grow your brand and your business.**

⇨BUILD YOUR BUSINESS EXERCISE: ACCOUNT STOCK AND OPTIMIZATION PREP

For this exercise, I recommend using the simple Account Optimization Sheet at SocialMediaOnAuto.com/Resources to help you organize and optimize your accounts.

Take stock of the accounts you have set up currently. Are these set up as business pages or personal profiles?

Using the information provided in the chapter, review your current accounts. Ask yourself:

- Do you need to create any new accounts?
- Are you missing any profiles? Which ones?

- How many followers on each existing account (how many followers on your Business Facebook account, for example)?
- Do they all contain the **exact same business name and business address** on all profiles? (Example: If you have one social media account set up with an address listed as "Ste 103", and another social media account or Google My Business page set up with the address listed as "Suite 103", this can hurt your reach and ranking views later.)

📷 FOCUS POINTS

In this chapter, we covered:

- The purpose of Social Media in Marketing (top of funnel)
- Why you should never buy followers, and what to do if you did
- ⇒Build Your Business Exercise: Social Media Account Audit
- ⇒Build Your Business Exercise: Calculate Your Engagement Score
- Personal accounts versus Business Page: Which is Right for You?
- ⇒Build Your Business Exercise: Account Stock and Optimization Prep

Please make sure you complete the exercises listed before moving on to the next chapter.

THREE
SEEING THE OPPORTUNITIES IN FRONT OF YOU—OVERTAKING THE COMPETITION USING SOCIAL MEDIA

If you discovered in the last chapter that you need to set up new accounts or that you need more social media accounts (maybe you have a personal Facebook profile but not a business Facebook Page)—great news!

Over the next few chapters, you're going to learn how to lay the foundation for your social channels the right way—the first time—so that you can automate your social media as quickly as possible.

Setting up accounts takes time to do it right, but once done, you will have assets that:

- Send social signals to search engines like Google on your behalf, to help you rank on search engine pages for search terms your prospects and customers are searching for—right now.
- Provide a space to test new offers on the mass market.
- Give potential customers a way to find you and existing customer to remember you.

- Move people off of social media and onto your website and email list.
- Position your brand name and service on the first page of a Google search.

Social media is about getting in front of your potential customers and existing customers where they are. For a lot of business owners that just want to "sell their services," the marketing side of owning a business can be a big headache, and let's be real, hiring a marketer or agency that actually knows what they're doing costs.

Entrepreneurs, agents, freelancers, and anyone in the early stages of developing their business are notorious for having the grit and gumption to try to DIY almost anything.

(Yes, I see you.)

For beginning or early businesses (a business under three years old or with fewer than five people working directly for you), if you want to set up and optimize your accounts yourself, setting up these particular accounts in the way I will show you will save you time, money, and headaches later.

If you are considering hiring an agency or marketer later, following the information in this chapter may help you avoid "new account setup and optimization fees" by having your accounts set up correctly the first time.

While I don't cover setup for every social media channel out there, you'll learn setup and optimization for the following major social media channels:

- Facebook
- Instagram
- LinkedIn

- Google My Business
- YouTube

I want to be upfront here. There is a solid bit of research initially. Estimate six to twelve hours of hands-on work for this next section. This is the same work I do for my clients, and it can last years if you take the time to do it right the first time.

As my dad told me growing up, "People never have time to do it right the first time, but they always make time to do it again."

Follow along with me, and you'll learn how to set up your initial social media strategy. This includes looking at the competition, coming up with initial "seed" keywords and hashtags for your posts, optimizing your pages, and learning about some recommended scheduling software that you (or your virtual assistant) can use to schedule content in batches to make work faster, easier, and more cost-effective.

Remember, this is a one-time expense of your time, working toward the goal of having an automated social media strategy that takes you less than two hours a month, giving you time freedom while growing your business.

If you currently don't have that time to develop your strategy or set up your accounts, reach out to me at SocialMediaOnAuto.com/Schedule to learn how my team and I can help you.

KNOW YOURSELF. KNOW YOUR COMPETITION.

In Chapter 1, you created a view of your ideal customer and your service arc. It's time to bring those back out and have them available for reference as you work through this next section.

You're going to analyze your competition to find their strengths and weaknesses so you can use that information to make decisions regarding your own content and brand. Having your service arc available during this next exercise can be handy, as you will likely see opportunities left open by your competition. Comparing these open areas to your service arc list will allow you to open yourself to opportunities to create products or services to fill those gaps for your clients and customers.

To do this, we'll use a simple marketing framework called a SWOT analysis. SWOT stands for strengths, weaknesses, opportunities, and threats. In marketing, we use this to review and look for areas of opportunity where we can overtake the competition. It's simple to learn and use. You may already know it. However, we're going to go more granular with this than you may have in the past.

Here's a SWOT analysis of a competitor's Facebook Page:

SWOT ANALYSIS - FACEBOOK

STRENGTHS	WEAKNESS
#2 in Facebook listing search for keyword and city (realtor Greenville, SC)	Videos posted on IG are cross-posted to Facebook. On Facebook, these videos have low engagement.
Uses keywords in "about" and "description" sections	
Posts 1x per day	Low engagement on Facebook posts in general.

OPPORTUNITIES	THREATS
Reference keywords used in "about" and "description" in my own FB "about" and "description" areas.	Loss of Facebook Page, it goes down (redirect all traffic from FB to website or email sign-up to mitigate this.)
Schedule posts 2x a day to overtake competition.	Algorithm could take weeks/months to show organic content.

As I'm using this matrix for a specific outcome, I've adapted how I use this tool a bit. In this analysis, the "Strengths" section represents the competitor's strengths on Facebook. I listed three strengths here, but there could be more. The "Weaknesses" section corresponds to the competitor's weaknesses as I see them on the Facebook platform. Their weaknesses allow me to spot opportunities for my Facebook account. I have listed opportunities for my account to overtake their account, or gain more traction for my business, in the "Opportunities" section. Finally, the "Threats" section is a space to list external factors that you cannot control. For example, if Facebook shuts down your account or the Facebook algorithm takes weeks or months to show your organic content, if at all.

There are ways to combat both of these external factors. If you are driving your most engaged followers to your website, or better yet, to your email list, you may be able to retarget them with ads from another platform (i.e., Google Ads) or email them—should Facebook shut down for any reason. In the event that Facebook takes too long to show your posts, you can set a budget to boost your most popular, engaging posts to reach more of your target audience for only a few dollars a day.

⇨ BUILD YOUR BUSINESS: KNOW YOUR COMPETITION: SWOT ANALYSIS

For this exercise, I recommend using the premade workbook available to you at SocialMediaOnAuto.com/Resources. If you don't have access to a printer right now, I want you to grab a pen and a few sheets of paper. You're going to create twelve SWOT analysis grids—four grids for each of your top three local competitors. Each competitor will have a grid for Facebook, Instagram, LinkedIn, and Google My Business.

While you can use this same strategy to SWOT analyze your competitor's YouTube accounts, for the purposes of this book and this strategy, we'll mostly be focused on Instagram and Google My Business, so analyzing YouTube is unnecessary at this time.

You should estimate spending ten to fifteen minutes per account per SWOT grid for this activity, or up to one and a half hours per competitor. If you don't get them all done in one sitting, don't worry, but make sure to complete them before moving on to the next activity.

Don't overthink it. Try to find three to four things you can put in each grid block—three to four observations on your competitor's Facebook strengths, then, three to four observations regarding their weaknesses on Facebook, etc.

If you'd like to get a more in-depth list of social media SWOT questions and would like to watch me go through a SWOT analysis in a video training, check out the course at SocialMediaOnAuto.com/Course.

Here is a summary list of questions to consider as you review the Facebook, Instagram, LinkedIn, and Google My Business profiles for each of your top three competitors.

- How many followers do they have?
- How many times do they post on this channel per week?
- What types of content are they posting?
- Are they posting the same content on all social media channels, or creating specific content for each channel? For example, is the same image on Facebook,

Instagram, and LinkedIn? Are they posting different types of content for each?
- What does the engagement look like on their content? Low? High?
- Are they posting at specific times? Recurring times?
- What keywords are they using?

Add these keywords to the "SEED Keywords" sheet of your Account Optimization Sheet in the column provided. You can use these as starter keywords in the next section.

- What hashtags are they using on their Instagram posts?

Add these "Opportunities" to the "SEED Hashtags" sheet in your Account Optimization Sheet. These will be your starter, or SEED hashtags. Between all three competitors, you should walk away from this exercise with a list of 40-50 SEED hashtags you can use later.

- Are they using branded highlights on their Instagram account for stories? (On an Instagram profile, these are the little circle icons that appear before the Instagram feed. The "feed" is where you scroll down to see the images or content being posted.)
- How many reviews do they have? This is important for Facebook and Google specifically, but can be helpful on LinkedIn as well. You'll want to write down the total number of reviews, as well as their average review rating (example 4.7 stars).

This is a lot of initial research, and I understand some people learn visually and audibly. If you would like to watch me perform a competitor review, over the shoulder style, please check out the course available with this book at SocialMediaOn Auto.com/Course to help you get started.

In this chapter, we have done a lot of work. We have dug deep to reveal opportunities that our competition has missed. Now that we have exposed opportunities, we want to use the right bait to attract our dream customers.

What bait? Why your own content and copy, of course.

⇨BUILD YOUR BUSINESS EXERCISE: CLIENT ATTRACTING CONTENT AUDIT

Now that you've identified a few opportunities, you need to check that those opportunities are in alignment with your ideal client in your target market. I'm going to walk you through a few strategies I use to identify key audiences for real estate photographers.

I recommend spending between fifteen and thirty minutes on this exercise.

Example Questions for Real Estate Photographers

> Take a look at your top five clients by revenue. Go check out their social media profiles.
>
> What are they posting? What is getting the most engagement?
>
> Why do you think those posts are getting the most engagement?
>
> Who would your realtor clients say are their top three competitors?

Go scope out their competitors' profiles.

What are they doing? What content are they posting? What's generating engagement?

Why do you need to know this?

Because this is how your potential clients—the realtors you want to work with—see and view social media.

These are the platforms they are on.

This is where they spend their time.

These are the types of content they like.

Now, it's time to audit yourself. This part can be tricky, but you need to put aside your personal bias and look at the numbers.

Look at your top three social media profiles. Your top three can be the ones you are running right now (the ones you're the most comfortable with).

1. Are your top three channels the same as your ideal audience's (realtors you want to work with)? (If you want to work with a realtor who utilizes Instagram a lot, is Instagram in the top three channels for your business?)
2. On Facebook, LinkedIn, and Instagram, search "real estate photographer YOUR CITY, STATE." Example: real estate photographer Austin, TX. Does your name pop up in the top search results? Whose does?

Take this time to think about your competition.

Are the same names you identified as the biggest competition in your local area the names that pop up in a search? Are they using SEO tactics on their profiles?

Analyze their content. What are they doing right? Where are there gaps? Are they posting regularly? Infrequently? Is their content branded? All over the place?

The idea here is that you want your content to be THE BEST content for THE AUDIENCE YOU WANT TO ATTRACT.

To use a fishing analogy, you gotta fish with the right bait.

If you're:

1. tailoring your content to create things that your audience already likes or loves to share (using bait—not just an empty hook in the water)
2. and if you're creating professional content (using quality bait—not just corn bits and food scraps)
3. and your VA is posting more on your pages than your competitor posts using the "dialed in" hashtag strategy I'll tell you more about in the next chapter (using multiple fishing rods with great bait on each one)

...well, you win the day.

A few small tweaks and a little bit of thoughtfulness are all it takes.

I have used this same framework (the SWOT analysis) to help everyone from small clients to coaching students to a Fortune 500 business create and test new offers, increase leads, stack offers, and increase revenue.

It is a simple framework that works. It is the beginning of learning how to use data to seize opportunities. By breaking down your top three competitors, channel by channel, you'll see the opportunities to serve your market that they are leaving unattended.

PRO TIP: If you find yourself in a slow season, take the time to run these exercises again. By looking for new market opportunities in slow seasons, you can do the work to build your new offers when it is slow, so that when the market is busy again, you're ready to take off!

📷 FOCUS POINTS

In this chapter, we covered:

- How to frame your competitor's weaknesses as opportunities for your business using the SWOT analysis and how to dissect your own content to see if it's in alignment with your ideal client, aka "how to fish with the right bait"
- ⇒Build Your Business: Know Your Competition —SWOT Analysis
- ⇒Build Your Business Exercise: Client Attracting Content Audit

There's only one step left before we optimize your current social media profiles and set up new accounts—creating your "Seed to Lead" keyword and hashtag lists to help you climb rank fast on search engines.

To get the maximum result from this book, I recommend not moving on to Chapter 4 until you've completed the competitor analysis and content audit work in this chapter.

FOUR
CREATING YOUR SEED KEYWORD AND HASHTAG LISTS

Question: Do you know where to hide something where no one will ever find it?

Answer: The second page of Google.

If you aren't familiar with the phrase "Google Local 3-pack," the 3-pack consists of the top three Google Maps listings of local businesses near you that offer services or products you are searching for. For small or local-based businesses, optimizing for this local listing can offer faster results than spending months optimizing a website using SEO.

When I started working on my husband's social media accounts, there was one thing I noticed pretty quickly—he wasn't in the Google Local 3-pack for his services—and I wanted to get him a "fast win."

After playing around with some free software and updating the name portion of his Google My Business profile, Ben was in the Google Local 3-pack in just 24 hours.

For our purposes, automating your social media marketing, building a well-known brand, and becoming the "go-to expert" for your service in your area are all goals of this book. But what good are lofty goals like that if your phone isn't ringing?

Keywords are important.

They are useful in both organic and paid traffic strategies used to generate traffic to your website and business for your company.

Keywords tell you a few things about your prospect—what they're thinking, where they are in the funnel, and can even give you clues about objections that you may need to overcome in your copy or on a sales call.

While this book focuses on automating social media following a proven strategy, knowing how to use a few keywords in your copy and how to update your Google My Business profile can bring you business now and help create recurring business for you in the future.

As such, in this chapter, you're going to learn how to find the keywords that people are using to search for services like yours right now, and also, how to translate those keywords into hashtags that you can use on Instagram to help you get your content in front of more people in your area—for free.

I call these two lists—my starter keywords and my starter hashtags—my "Seeds to Leads" lists. I cultivate them as one would cultivate seeds, which, when planted and cared for, grow into a beautiful garden.

The difference is that these seeds will grow your business by helping new customers find you easily.

BASIC KEYWORD AND HASHTAG RESEARCH: KEYWORD SEED LIST

How To Find Keywords For Your Business

Keyword research is actually pretty simple. And thankfully, there are a lot of great programs you can use to find your first five to ten keywords around which to focus your website, copy, and hashtag strategy.

I've listed a few of my favorite keyword tools below, along with the current prices. The prices below are correct as of the time of the publication of this book. They are obviously subject to change.

Here are a few of my favorite programs and tools:

FREE keyword software programs (meaning—they're going to try to sell you something while you're there and you get a limited number of keyword searches per day):

Ubersuggest by Neil Patel

- $29 per month for the upgraded account.
- 3 searches per day limit on the free account

KWFinder by Mangools

- $49 per month with a few more features
- 10-Day Free Trial

Keyword Magic Tool by SEMRUSH

- $119 per month
- 7-Day Free Trial

MOZ Keyword Explorer

- $99 per month
- 30-Day Free Trial

AnswerThePublic

- $99 per month for the Pro Account
- Free

Google Trends

- Free

Google Search Console

- If you already have this hooked up your website—great! You can view the search terms that are driving clicks to your website using Search Console.

People Also Ask:

- $39 per month
- Free to try

For what you'll be doing, you don't need to buy any of these. Just the trial will do. Just remember to download your results from your searches and save them for later!

⇨BUILD YOUR BUSINESS EXERCISE: INITIAL SEED KEYWORD BANK

Choose one of the services above to get started. I'm partial to Ubersuggest because it is very user-friendly.

Open the software, and watch a tutorial on how to search within it for keywords. Depending on the software you choose, the website may offer a "quick tour" option, or you can search for a five-minute tutorial on YouTube. I recommend only spending five to ten minutes here to familiarize yourself with the software and functionality. Set a timer and don't get distracted!

A Note On Long Tail Keywords

You'll be searching long tail keywords for your keyword list.

Long-tail keywords, also called keyword phrases, tell search engines how to find the best results for a search. As you are searching for keywords inside your preferred keyword software, use longtail keyword phrases to help you search for relevant search terms, just as you would search for services at home.

Instead of searching "real estate" or "real estate photographer", which are shorter keyword phrases, try searching long tail keyword phrases like "real estate photographer Louisville, KY" or "best real estate agent Santa Rosa". One of the best things about long tail keywords is that they indicate user intent.

People who use long tail keywords are further down the sales funnel, and more ready to make a purchasing decision than someone who searches generic terms like "photographer New York." Go specific. Go long tail.

Get Started Searching!

Open your Keyword Search Tool and enter in keywords that you would use naturally to search for your product or service.

A list will appear in your software, usually featuring an exact match of your keyword phrase, plus a few recommendations that you may not have considered.

The key is to look for keywords that are (1) relevant to your business and make sense, (2) have moderate to high search volume, and (3) have low organic competition scores (i.e., are easier to rank for). You want to identify ten to fifteen keywords that have higher search volume and lower competition scores.

Each SEO software will show this a little differently in their search results view, but typically, you'll get something like this:

KEYWORD IDEAS

KEYWORD	VOLUME	CPC	PD	SD
Real Estate Agent Greenville SC	320	$8.20	63	59
Real Estate Agent In Greenville SC	390	$10.81	80	30
Real Estate Agencies In Greenville SC	320	$8.20	63	44
Real Estate Agencies Greenville SC	320	$8.20	63	46
Real Estate Agent Greenville South Carolina	320	$8.20	63	61
Top Real Estate Agent In Greenville SC	50	$5.20	92	56
Top Real Estate Agents In Greenville SC	50	$11.37	97	56

Notice how, in the second option, "Real Estate Agent in Greenville SC" has:

- a higher search volume: 390 searches per month
- a cost per click of $10.81. This is the estimated price you'd pay if you were to use this particular longtail keyword in a Google Ads campaign. Ubersuggest estimates it will cost you $10.81 to get people to click your ad using this keyword in your ad. Typically, a

- higher cost per click means the view is closer to making a purchasing decision.
- a PD, or paid search difficulty of 80, meaning it's very hard to rank for and a lot of people are throwing money at this keyword in ads to get people to click to their page
- but, the organic search difficulty score is only 30. This lower score is generally easier to rank on Google. The lower the SD score (search difficulty score), the easier it is to rank.

What does all that mean?

This keyword phrase is a high-value, highly sought-after keyword, likely due to the intent of the searcher. Since everyone is fighting over paid ads but few know how to use organic keywords well, you could rank for this keyword organically with just a little effort. Using the specific keyword phrase in your website copy, social media profiles, and scheduled social media posts could rank you on page one of Google—without ever spending a dime on paid ads.

The only downside to organic keywords? They take time to grow. It's a bit like farming. That is why your first list of keywords is called your "SEED list." We start with these and an initial strategy to get your social media automated and off your plate.

While these "seeds" are growing with the help of your virtual assistant (who will be posting your content for you following this system), you'll be focusing on other aspects of your business. In the background, your Social Media on Auto strategy will be hard at work, gaining you rank on Google and building you up as the "go-to expert" for your city or location.

Now, go find your initial fifteen to twenty SEED Keywords and list them in your Account Optimization Sheet in the column titled "Keywords from Keyword Search" on the SEED Keywords tab.

When we dive into optimizing your existing accounts and creating new ones in the next chapter, you'll refer back to this keyword list to update copy, account names, and more. For now, simply make a list of your top keywords (copying them exactly as they appear in the software search results) and list them in your Account Optimization Sheet.

Prefer to learn visually? Watch me go through and research more keywords using the tools I've mentioned above in the video training I recorded for you at SocialMediaOnAuto.com/Course.

FLICK AND HASHTAG RESEARCH

Hashtags in Instagram work a bit like keywords in Google. Hashtags offer the algorithm a way to describe and categorize the photo and offer users a way to search for similar content.

I currently spend more time watching Instagram analytics than Facebook or other social media platforms. There are a few reasons.

My clients, real estate photographers, are blessed with a never-ending stream of content that works well on Instagram. If they're good photographers, I have a steady stream of content to work with to help them rank.

Demographically, according to a 2018 Statista report, over 60 percent of Instagram users are pulling in over $100,000 a year. In comparison, according to a 2019 Pew Report, teens from lower-income households are more likely to use Facebook than teens from higher-income households. Instagram is also easier to rank on, as it is generally easier to get higher engagement on Instagram than Facebook. (Because what's the point of doing any work at all on social media if no one will see it?)

I concentrate on growing my clients' Instagram accounts—growing the space where their clients (realtors) and clients' clients (higher income homeowners) hang out—with a slew of images that work for that platform, using keywords and curated hashtags to drive views, followers, and revenue. When Instagram is growing, the other channels (Facebook, LinkedIn, YouTube, and even Google My Business) all follow suit.

That's why you need to have a basic working knowledge of hashtags. Hashtags are a key component in solving for Instagram. Ranking content and growing a brand on Instagram is like solving a five-part equation, where each portion of the equation affects the result, or how much reach your post will get.

Think of it this way:

> Content Quality + Content Relevance + Copy/Caption + Hashtags + Time of Post = Audience Reach

Having a collection of well-performing hashtags can help you reach larger audiences, grow your following faster, and help you grow your business. But how do you know which hashtags to use on your posts?

Simple. Flick will tell you.

You are going to get started with a new account on one of my favorite hashtag analytics softwares, Flick Tech. You'll sign up for a new account, go through a bit of free video training from their training library, and then follow my Local Thirds Strategy to create your hashtag collections. These are lists of hashtags you will use on your posts to increase your reach and gain new followers and new business.

After running the Local Thirds Strategy for your first thirty days, you'll hand over the hashtag collections you've curated and access to your Flick dashboard to a virtual assistant who will find new hashtags for you, post your content, and help keep an eye on ranking analytics and reports, while you focus on the other parts of your business.

Note: Account Growth Expectations

Using my Local Thirds Strategy, you should expect to grow your Instagram following anywhere from 50 to 250 +/- locally targeted, engaged followers the first month, depending on your ability to watch, learn, and pivot your strategy quickly, your current Instagram following size, and the population size of the metro area you're targeting.

⇨BUILD YOUR BUSINESS EXERCISE: HASHTAG SOFTWARE AND TRAINING

Open your Account Optimization Sheet in a new tab. Next, sign up for a Flick.tech account. Flick is my preferred hashtag research and analytics software for many reasons, including ease of use, competitive pricing, and their amazing (currently free) training.

Once inside, search for their free Instagram hashtag course. It's currently listed on their main homepage under Flick Academy. The entire course is about an hour and a half long, but don't worry; you don't need to go through the full course, only the first few modules. The course offers a simple introduction to hashtag strategy and also serves as a great tutorial on how to navigate the software that you will use for Instagram analytics.

Visit tinyurl.com/flicktrial for free starter credits and a free trial of Flick.tech.

The Flick training course is so well done that there's really no need for me to attempt to replicate it in this book. It's the very course I put my own VAs through as part of their introductory training with me. I'm going to recommend that you go through a few of the modules, watching the videos, so that you understand the basics of Instagram hashtag strategy as well as how to use the software before applying my Local Thirds Strategy, which I break down later in this chapter.

For now:

- Open your Account Optimization Sheet in a new tab, so that you have access to your long tail keywords and competitor hashtags.
- Create your Flick.tech account.
- Watch "Module One: Establish" through "Module Three: Hashtags" in the Instagram training course, paying special attention to the hashtag strategy covered for new accounts, small accounts, etc., in Module Three.

IMPORTANT: While you watch Module Two, keep in mind, this training for this module was created for larger accounts. Do not create any of the Collections taught in Module Two or Module Three. In my Local Thirds Strategy, you'll learn a variation of the Small Account Strategy covered in Module Three, which I've tailored for targeted local market reach and domination.

- After you've watched Modules 1-3 of the Flick Training, continue on to the next Build Your Business Exercise: The Local Thirds Strategy.

⇨ BUILD YOUR BUSINESS EXERCISE: LOCAL THIRDS STRATEGY —A MODIFIED SMALL ACCOUNT STRATEGY FOR LOCAL MARKETS

In Module Three of the free Instagram hashtag course in Flick, the course instructors ask you to start compiling hashtag lists, called Collections, in Flick. The goal is to have sixty hashtags that you can use to begin posting.

This is a great strategy if you are looking for national exposure. However, if you have a local, service-based business or are targeting local markets, I recommend a slight variation if you're new to Instagram or just getting started.

> I recommend using my Local Thirds Strategy.

In Instagram, you can include up to thirty hashtags per post. By breaking these thirty hashtags down into three categories, you can test a mix of ten hashtags per category, per post.

I have found the following categories work well for small businesses and new accounts getting started—industry, photo description, and location.

For industry-specific hashtags, you might try:

> #realtorlife, #dronephotographer, #photoshop, or #sellrealestate.

For property description or photo description hashtags, you could describe the property or photo using hashtags like:

> #finishedbasement, #marblecounters, or #diningdecor.

The local hashtags are usually the easiest to find as they are the ones typically used for your market area, for example:

#CharlotteNC

In this Build Your Business Exercise, you will use your previous hashtag research from your SWOT competitor analysis and your long-tail keyword research to compile three collections of curated hashtags using the Local Thirds Strategy.

You'll be taking the hashtags you've already found plus the keywords you discovered and running them through a filtered search in Flick to find starter hashtags for your first thirty days.

"But why can't I just get started using the hashtags from my competitors?" you may ask.

You could try. But depending on your skill level with copy, the health of your account, and the quality of your content, some of those competitor hashtags may be too hard for you to rank for yet. However, by entering those competitive hashtags into the Flick Hashtags research tool and then setting the filters I recommend, you'll get a list of hashtags in low competition, medium competition, and high competition categories that you could rank for.

First, create three new collections in Flick. You may want to name them Industry, Description, and Location to keep it simple.

Then, set search filters in Flick using the recommendations below. Next, copy and paste your long-tail keywords and your competitor's hashtags, one at a time, in the search bar to search for hashtags in Flick. Using the filters below will allow you to filter out lower-competition hashtags that will not help you much as you get started.

While searching for your first hashtags, apply the following filters to your search to filter out lower competition hashtags that will not help you much.

- On your Total Posts filter, set the minimum for 5,000 (meaning the hashtag has been used in at least 5,000 posts) and set the maximum to 50,000.
- For the Average Daily Likes filter, set your minimum to 125 and your maximum to 350, so that the hashtags you see are, on average, used on posts that generate at least 125-350 likes per day.

As you search for hashtags to add to your collections, try to only choose hashtags that could work for your brand (remembering to preview content from other accounts that use those hashtags as you learned how to do in the Flick video tutorials). Hashtags that work for your brand and your brand image should be added to the appropriate collection (i.e., #realestatephotographer would go into the "Industry" collection).

If you feel confused or unsure about whether you should put a hashtag in the "Industry" or "Photo Description" collection, try thinking about it this way. "Industry" collection hashtags resemble search terms you might search on Google to find someone who offers your service.

The "Photo Description or Property Description" collection will be where you save and test hashtags that describe what is in the photo. Think about hashtags like "#sunsetproperty" or "#justlisted."

Need a little help? Feel free to refer to the list of hashtags you scraped from your competitor research. Can you see using some of these more than others? Look them up in Flick and add them to your collection. After all, there's no point in reinventing the wheel and banging your head against the wall if your competitor has done a solid bit of work in advance. You can use their work and still find new creative hashtags to play with as you learn and grow.

By the end of this exercise, you should have twenty hashtags in each of the three collections. Make sure you have a mix of low and medium competition in each collection.

You now have sixty hashtags you can use to test on your first month's posts!

Remember, you don't have to be instantly amazing at hashtags and ranking every post out of the gate. The first month or two are all about collecting data and learning the software and your audience. You start out with hashtags you think will work, and focus on being consistent with posting to your social media accounts. Slow and steady wins the race. Fast is good, unless you burn out. Consistency, however, always wins.

⇨BUILD YOUR BUSINESS EXERCISE: 30 HASHTAGS FOR "ON-THE-GO"

While the goal of this book is to create an automated system that you hand off to someone else to manage for you, you should understand the process enough to know if they're doing a good job, or just taking your money and getting you bad results. You should also be ready (and feel empowered and inspired) to post a great shot from your phone on the go.

After all, social media should be fun.

I like for clients to have a deck of on-the-go, battle-tested hashtags that they can pull out of their pocket and just copy/paste from the "Notes" section of their phone in the event that they are lined up for that perfect shot or video.

The "on-the-go" list is a mix of hashtags using ten to fifteen location hashtags, ten to fifteen industry or relevant hashtags, and space for five to ten additional "community" or "event" hashtags.

Take an extra 5–10 minutes now and create a list of 30 hashtags that you can copy and email yourself so that you have them pocket-ready, on your phone, for when you find yourself in an opportunistic moment and want to post immediately.

Pro Tip: Make sure to include your brand's hashtag as the first hashtag in your list to help increase your brand's exposure!

FOCUS POINTS

Before you move on to the next chapter, you should:

- Have created your SEED keyword list
- Have created your three collections in Flick following the Local Thirds Strategy.
- Have thirty "on-the-go" hashtags saved to your notepad on your phone for posting on Instagram on the go.

FIVE
CREATING NEW ACCOUNTS & OPTIMIZING YOUR CURRENT ACCOUNTS TO RANK ON GOOGLE AND OTHER SEARCH ENGINES

If you're posting content but not getting the results you want—it could be that you don't have your accounts set up correctly. If you discovered in Chapter 2 that you need to create a few new accounts, or you know you could be getting more ROI from your current social media—this is your chapter.

Part of the *Social Media on Auto* strategy involves distributing and scheduling social media content on various platforms, all at the same time.

The goal is focused on ranking and growing Instagram primarily, as all your other channels will grow along with it.

In order to get the maximum return out of your efforts, I want you to optimize your social media accounts for search engine optimization. To do that, we need to revamp your profiles so that search engines can crawl your social media profiles more easily and recommend your social media accounts to people searching for your product or service.

Done correctly, you can essentially count each of your social media accounts as another free "web page" pointing to your business. In fact, you can have multiple first-page listings on a Google search for your keywords.

Imagine searching for the "best real estate agent in Albany NY" and finding three first page listings for your business.

There is only space on the first page of Google for three Google local listings at the top of the page. Below that, Google may show up to eight organic search engine results, depending on the number of paid ads at the top of the page. If your agency has three listings on page one, your business owns over 27 percent of the first page real estate for a search containing the "best real estate agent in Albany, NY". For every one person that searches that search term, you have more than a one in four chance of that person clicking on your social media account or your website to learn more about you.

That's why you're going to optimize your social media profiles. You could walk away with extra clients, customers, or listings for your business simply by appearing on page one of Google search results. As an added bonus, optimizing your social media accounts boosts the signal that is sent from social media sites to your website. This helps boost your website's overall domain authority, which can help your website rank better in search results for key terms as well. It's a win-win-win all around.

⇨ BUILD YOUR BUSINESS EXERCISE: MIGRATING TO NEW ACCOUNTS

A Note on Replacing Tainted Accounts

If you have tainted accounts and need to create new ones, start by backing up any data you have on the tainted accounts.

Download a copy of your data from the social media platform. You can download a copy of your data from Facebook, LinkedIn, and Instagram. This will allow you to go back through and re-add friends or followers that you recognize, as well as potentially download any photos or videos you have on these accounts to reupload later.

You will also want to schedule a date in the near future that you plan to delete the old accounts.

During the time between now and the date you will delete your tainted accounts, **make sure to replace any links to your old social media accounts (for example, the footer links in your website) or set up redirects BEFORE you delete the tainted accounts.** It is best practice to replace as many of the links to your old accounts manually, as opposed to setting up redirects, as possible. This will prevent potential issues with 301 redirects later.

⇨BUILD YOUR BUSINESS EXERCISE: OPTIMIZING YOUR FACEBOOK PAGE

In the following exercise, you will learn how to optimize your business' Facebook Page for search engines. Once you have optimized your Facebook Page, you will apply the same ideas and concepts to each of your other social media profiles and your Google My Business profile, using your Account Optimization Sheet available with this book to guide you.

> Pro-Tip: Enter your information (keywords, address, etc.) in the Account Optimization Spreadsheet first, then copy it over into your Facebook Page. This will save you time later. After optimizing your Facebook Page, you can easily copy the information from your spreadsheet over to your other social accounts, in similar or appropriate areas.

Facebook Page Name

One of the fastest and best ways to get more SEO juice (and visitors) to your social media accounts is to include your root keyword in the name of your business page. Your main keyword or keyword phrase should be the one you are most likely to rank for with the highest traffic count possible.

Refer to the list of long-tail keywords you compiled in the ⇒**Build Your Business Exercise: Initial SEED Keyword Bank** you completed in Chapter 4. Google will pick up your city or area name (for example, "Greenville, SC") from your physical location, as well as any time your city or area name is mentioned in the "About—Details" section of your Facebook Page. Because of this, your Facebook Page name only needs to contain the root keyword. Refer to the graphic below.

KEYWORD IDEAS

KEYWORD	VOLUME	CPC	PD	SD
Real Estate Agent Greenville SC	320	$8.20	63	59
Real Estate Agent In Greenville SC	390	$10.81	80	30
Real Estate Agencies In Greenville SC	320	$8.20	63	44
Real Estate Agencies Greenville SC	320	$8.20	63	46
Real Estate Agent Greenville South Carolina	320	$8.20	63	61
Top Real Estate Agent In Greenville SC	50	$5.20	92	56
Top Real Estate Agents In Greenville SC	50	$11.37	97	56

The root keyword from the phrase "Real Estate Agent In Greenville SC" would be "Real Estate Agent".

Let's look at another example. Let's say you own a real estate photography business named "DRIVE Drone Photography." You discover from your research that the keyword phrase "real estate photography" is the main keyword for your business. By editing your Facebook Page name to something like "DRIVE Drone Real Estate Photography," you snag more traffic to your Facebook Page from search engine results. From your Facebook Page, prospects can engage with your content and navigate to your website to book your services.

Use Your Top 5-10 Keywords On Your Page

In addition to your main keyword listed in your Page or profile name, you'll want to include any similar keywords in the available "About" or "Services" sections of your page. Examples would include keywords like "realtor," "seller agent," or "real estate photographer."

A few great places to include your secondary keywords are your:

- Bio
- Page Category
- Headline
- Banner Image Graphic (and in the image description)
- Photo captions and photo ALT text (where available—this is GOLD in Instagram posts and Google My Business posts)
- "About" section. For this section, try to keep your description of your business and services to less than 300 characters. Use your primary and secondary keywords, keep it punchy, and explain why customers love you! For example, "Drive Drone offers real estate photography—drone and aerial photos—in Phoenix, Arizona. We are 5-Star rated and offer 48-hour turnaround on projects!"

Remember, focus on using the top five to ten keywords you identified from your previous keyword research in the copy in these sections to get more eyes on your page and your posts!

Grab Your Custom URL and "@" Name

Many social channels allow you to have a custom vanity URL and tag name for your business. If you haven't already, make sure to customize both of these.

Using "Drive Drone Photography" as an example for a vanity URL, we could use facebook.com/dridedronerealestatephotography or facebook.com/drive-drone-real-estate-photography, to get our keywords in, all while informing anyone who visits that Facebook Page what the company offers.

Your custom "@", mention, or tag name is a great option to increase branding and allow people to tag your company in photos as well. Generally, this custom "@" name should be short and sweet. Believe me when I say, no one wants to type thirty plus characters to tag your business in a photograph or post.

To keep things simple, for Drive Drone Photography, I would likely just claim @drivedrone or maybe @drivedronephotography.

In this example, the second option is better because it includes a service keyword—photography. While it doesn't contain the full keyword, it does tell the person viewing the photo and the business tagged in the photo what "Drive Drone" does—photography. This can be enough to encourage viewers to click on the tag name and visit the business profile page.

Business Information

For every page you set up in the future, always use the **EXACT same business information.**

To make this easy to track and manage, use the "Address" section on the "Account Prep" tab of your Account Optimization Sheet to list your business phone and address, keeping all your address listings and phone numbers formatted exactly the same for each listing or profile you have online.

Where possible, like on Facebook and Yelp, make sure to include other relevant information such as business hours, parking, if you serve customers at your location or theirs, and, if you feel comfortable with it, pricing (usually this is in the form of "$-$$$$" symbols).

Set Your CTA Button

The Call to Action section of your Facebook Page is where you can customize the big button at the top of the page. Here, you point your audience to the action that you want them to take.

Common CTAs for Facebook include: Message, Get Quote, or Learn More. If you're not sure which CTA to use, I recommend using "Learn More" to start. "Learn More" is generally linked to your business website and is a great way to get curious prospects over to your website to learn more about your business.

Design

When updating your page for search engines, you also want to update your page to include branded banners for your Facebook and LinkedIn business pages that don't focus on "what you do," but instead focus on the problem you solve for your dream customers and your unique angle in your industry. Offer your audience a quick, visual landing place for their eyes to rest while learning more about you and how you can help them.

Make sure all your account banners and images have a branded, cohesive look. If you don't have a graphic designer on your team you can use, you can find someone on a site like Fiverr to design things for you, or try to design your own banners yourself in a design software like Canva.

A word of caution here: If you are not a designer or don't have a natural knack for design, don't try to design your own graphics. It will hurt your brand image more than you know.

Instead, start by purchasing a basic brand kit for your business from a qualified graphic designer. Your brand kit is a reflection of your business; make sure it looks professional. A well-designed brand kit typically includes two to four brand colors, both main and complementary colors, as well as a few fonts for your business and brand. Brand kits can be created to match or complement your existing logo or even serve as a starting point for a future logo design.

Brand kits are typically delivered as a PDF or presentation file that you can save and reference again and again as you design images in the future. Your brand kit or brand guidelines will help you, and your future content creators and virtual assistants, all stay on brand with your images and messaging in the future. Skipping this step can result in a messy, confusing visual for your prospects, and headaches later for you, so don't skip it.

As you begin to upload your new banners and brand images, you may see a space to enter ALT text for each image you upload. ALT text is descriptive text used by search engines to help web bots know what the photo or image on the page is about, so that they can show relevant images to users in searches. Make sure to add ALT text to your banner images and name your banner images something from your keyword set, for example "Katie Sue McIntosh—realtor and real estate investor—Dallas, Texas."

It is important not to use the same ALT text for every photo or banner you upload. Use your main keyword for your main banner images and swap out your secondary keywords in any supporting images that you use in your profile. Make sure that any ALT text used describes the image shown. Trying to include keywords in ALT text spaces that do not match the image on screen is an example of keyword stuffing and is looked down upon by search engines.

After doing all this work, the last thing you want to do is earn negative SEO points on your social media accounts by trying to use the ALT text field to label a photo you took of an apple with your keyword to try to outsmart search engines. Artificial intelligence will figure it out and nick you for it later. Instead, take photos that represent you, your business, and your brand and then use your long tail keyword phrases in the ALT text.

After completing the optimization of your Facebook Page, you will use the same steps and strategies to set up or optimize your:

- LinkedIn business page
- WhatsApp business page—this is a new*er* platform for many US-based businesses. Currently, Facebook allows you to connect your Facebook Page to your WhatsApp business page.
- Instagram account bio
- YouTube profile
- and Google My Business Page.

INSTAGRAM SPECIFIC TIP: HOW TO USE YOUR KEYWORDS IN YOUR INSTAGRAM BIO

On your Instagram profile, a great place to put keywords is your bio. Instagram currently limits bios to 150 characters or less, so make sure to include one or two of your highest value keywords. I recommend choosing a highly searched keyword phrase that includes your service, location or city, and state.

Connect your Instagram Business Profile to your Facebook Page

After completing the optimization of your Facebook Page, you're ready to connect your Facebook Page to your Instagram business profile. Connecting accounts will allow you to seamlessly share content between both platforms, making posting for your business a cinch later while also offering better analytics of your audience and your accounts.

However, if you haven't set up your Instagram business profile yet or need to convert a personal profile into a business profile (recommended only if your personal profile is only used to promote your business), you will need to create your Instagram business profile first and then circle back to this step to connect the two accounts.

To connect your Facebook and Instagram accounts, go to your Facebook Professional Dashboard and then navigate to Linked Accounts. Follow the steps on the screen to connect your Facebook Page, Instagram business profile, and WhatsApp business accounts.

📷 FOCUS POINTS

In this chapter, you learned to optimize your Facebook Page for more free search traffic and more conversions. Before you move onto the next chapter, take this time to set up and optimize ALL your social media accounts.

This process could take between forty-five minutes to a few hours, depending on your comfort with the various platforms, implementation speed, and overall organization of business data.

Here are a few tips to simplify and speed up the process for you:

- Organize your address and other important information in your Account Optimization Sheet before beginning to optimize your accounts. This will help keep all your information the same for each platform as you optimize.
- Take a tour of your business Facebook Page first. Spend ten to twenty minutes familiarizing yourself with the Edit/Settings section and Professional Dashboard in Facebook. This will help you move faster as you enter your address, phone number, and keywords to optimize your account.
- Done is better than perfect. If you have to have no banner at all on your business pages for now, that is fine. Just keep setting up and optimizing your accounts using what you do have—your keyword research and matching address and phone number information.

As a reminder, these are the accounts you need to set up and optimize. Check them off as you complete them.

- Facebook Page
- Instagram business profile
- Remember to connect your Facebook Page to your Instagram business account.
- Google My Business Page
- LinkedIn Personal Profile
- YouTube account (if you have one)

So far, you have learned how to perform keyword research for your business, the basics of Instagram hashtag strategy, and the Local Thirds Strategy to help you take over the market in your area. You have also applied what you learned by optimizing your social media profiles to get more eyeballs on your brand and more clicks to your website.

The next step is posting content. In the following chapters, you'll learn how much content you really need, how to recycle content to save your sanity, and how to hand it all off to someone else to manage for you while you relax.

SIX
HELPING OTHERS

The purpose of this book is to help others experience the freedom I have found through automating social media marketing, freeing up more time for activities I and my family enjoy while growing businesses.

Imagine not being tied to a social media calendar, worrying about what to post and when, and trying to watch analytics dashboards day in and day out. Imagine watching your business grow while you work "on" your business, not "in" your business.

We all know word-of-mouth marketing is one of the most ROI-positive marketing methods you can invest in for your business, but many people, just like you, simply don't know how to execute it well.

Millions of entrepreneurs and sole proprietors are exhausted every day trying to "hack" word-of-mouth marketing. They attend too many networking events, create random social media posts, and print flyers and unending coupons for services.

While all of these methods can be profitable, they can also burn out a business owner who is already doing everything they can to grow their business.

By automating *part* of the equation of word-of-mouth marketing—the part that produces the greatest reward from the sheer number of people reached—business owners reduce the time, energy, and effort it takes to grow their businesses. They reclaim some of their life force for other positive endeavors and begin taking time to relax and enjoy life. After all, we only get one life...

There is no doubt that you know someone else, someone a lot like you, perceivably burning the candle at both ends, trying to fit it all into a 12 to 16-hour work day, and who is feeling exhausted by the simple idea of waking up in the morning only to repeat the cycle.

You know someone, like you, who wants a real business—something you can take vacations from and come back to—with the business still growing and thriving.

While there are many steps to this process, this book offers solutions to two parts of this equation:

1. Branding your business so that you can grow in any economy
2. Automating processes that take up your time so that you can focus on higher-leveraged activities, like testing new offers.

This book contains 12+ years of digital marketing knowledge, with step-by-step plays of the steps you need to implement to succeed—without selling you 15 things you don't need.

If you are finding this book helpful (and I hope you are), I have one small favor to ask that will take you less than a minute of your time.

Leave a review for this book.

In doing so, you will help hundreds to thousands of other small business owners, just like yourself, take one more step toward exiting the rat race that causes so many to give up on their dreams before they realize them.

One minute of your time could change someone's life trajectory.

One minute of your time could save a business owner from untold stress that causes them to give up on their dream and put themselves and the family they are providing for back into the "job" economy.

You remember why you started your own business. They have a similar story to yours.

In this selfless act of helping someone else, you are exercising your personal choice to put out good energy and vibes into the world.

Leaving a review is simple.

To leave a review on Kindle or your e-reader, scroll or page-flip to the end of this book, where you will be prompted to leave a review.

To leave a review on Amazon (or whatever site you purchased this book from), search for the book title on the platform where you purchased the book, sign in, and leave your review there.

Thank you for your help and time.

📷 FOCUS POINTS

I wanted to take this opportunity to note that you're more than halfway finished building out your *Social Media on Auto* processes!

Take a moment to celebrate how far you've come!

Since starting this book, you have:

- learned how social media functions as a marketing tool,
- learned where social media fits into your business marketing (primarily at the top of the funnel/branding objectives),
- set up top-performing social media and Google My Business accounts,
- learned how to analyze and evaluate your competition and your market area to see opportunities that others have missed,
- learned how to hone in on your services and your audience (target customers) to help create new offers to better serve them and your market,
- learned how to test new angles in your marketing to position yourself as "the go-to expert" for your area of expertise,
- learned how to perform initial keyword and hashtag research to grow your business' reach without spending money on ads,
- and also learned how to optimize your social media pages using keywords and hashtags to grow your reach exponentially faster while maintaining a local focus.

You have learned and executed more in five chapters than many university students learn in a few years of focused marketing study, and what you learned and implemented is not theory but actionable, helping you grow your business while relieving you of future stress and freeing up your time.

Take a moment now to celebrate your progress before moving onto the next chapter, where you'll begin building the systems you'll be running for content automation and social media domination.

SEVEN
HOW MUCH CONTENT DO I REALLY NEED?

When I tell realtors and real estate photographers that they don't have to go and create millions of pieces of content to use the Social Media on Auto strategy, they're puzzled.

How?

I mean, every other Facebook or Instagram ad is telling them to download or buy my "365 days of content calendar" so you can create content for your audience every day!

I get it. I do. I used to do stuff like that also.

But gah, was it ever EXHAUSTING. Can you relate?

So, how much content do you really need?

This depends on your goals. If you're in a position where you constantly have access to new content, use what you have!

If you're looking for a number, one to three posts per day is a great start.

Now, you may think, "One to three times per day?" "How am I going to produce that much content?" Don't worry; I have a system for you.

Do I have to make videos? I hate being on camera.

First, I would challenge your thinking on that idea. Maybe you don't hate ALL videos. For example, I don't enjoy face-to-camera or "talking head" videos of myself. I don't enjoy being the focal point of the video.

I get anxious. I worry that I talk too much. The lighting is wrong. My audio is off. You can see the ring light reflection in my glasses. You get the point.

However, when I am teaching over-the-shoulder strategies, I don't mind being on camera at all.

Why?

The video is not about me. It's about serving people where they are. Their eyes are on my screen, watching me move from item to item. They are not solely focused on me. They can see me, which builds trust, but I am not the focal point.

Consider this. It may not be being on video that you hate, but how you've been told you have to use video for your business. If you've been told you have to do Instagram reels and TikTok and Facebook Lives, and while those things can help some businesses—they don't help everyone. If you're uncomfortable on camera, it shows.

Another type of video I love creating is a customer testimonial or case study interview. I love personal accomplishment stories. Who doesn't? It's great when you can see someone overcome obstacles to hit a goal or accomplish a dream. In these types of videos, I am not anxious because the customer or client is the focus of the story, not the interviewer.

In addition to teaching and interview videos, other types of videos that you can create that do not require you to be the focus of the video include behind-the-scenes videos of your team, videos of your service or product and the production of that service or product, or (and this is an easy one for real estate agents) real estate videos of the houses that you are listing.

What content sells?

What content doesn't sell? Every piece of content sells your business or service. Whether you are selling your brand, your service, your trustworthiness, your general likability, or your customer success rate, every piece sells.

That said, there are a few types of content that I consistently recommend for businesses of any type and size. They are: behind-the-scenes meet the team spotlight, community shots, customer testimonials, and services.

For "services" content, it may be helpful to think in categories. For real estate photographers, I use categories like interior shots, exterior shots, aerial shots, twilight shots, detail shots, Matterport videos, before and after photos, virtual staging, floor plans, and sky swaps.

Think about the different services your business offers. When you can, pair your image with a bit of copy showcasing results. Sometimes adding text like "Sold in under 24 hours" performs even better!

You might be amazed to find out what types of content your audiences respond to the most.

⇨BUILD YOUR BUSINESS EXERCISE: SETTING UP YOUR CONTENT FOLDERS

In order to share your photos and videos with your current or future virtual assistant, you'll want to organize your content into a cloud-based storage solution, such as Google Drive or Dropbox.

I suggest choosing a cloud-based storage option that is easily accessible on your mobile phone, in case you need to make edits when away from your computer.

Take some time to choose your storage application and set up any sharing permissions that will help you manage your folders.

Now, create a folder. This will be your main storage folder. Name it "Social Media Content."

Create these content subfolders. I've given example content below each folder heading where some clarification might be needed.

1. BTS—Behind the Scenes

Example content includes:

- Posing a tripod on top of your car to get the perfect shot
- That day, you accidentally spilled coffee on your shirt, but thank God your camera was dry!
- A ziploc bag around your camera you tried once when shooting exteriors on a rainy day
- Photos of you editing photos

2. MTT—Meet The Team

These photos are a great way to showcase your people and bring faces to your feed.

3. Community Shots

Photos of you and your team members celebrating your community are great for showing that you know your community better than anyone. When volunteering or attending events, these photos can also showcase that you are a stable force for good in your community and neighborhood.

4. Services or Products

This is the folder where you'll save photos of your services or products. If sharing product photos, remember to make sure your photographs are aesthetically pleasing. Some photographers specialize in product photography, or you can look into free or inexpensive courses online to learn how to take great product photos with your phone.

5. Problem/Solution Posts

This photo category is pretty simple. Show the problem, then show you offering the solution! Refer to the work you did in "They Got Fifty Problems" for content ideas!

An idea for a problem/solution post for a real estate photographer could include a before/after photo layout featuring an exterior shot of a home before and after a grass swap.

Don't have visual before and after images to show? Test a few copy only images. Imagine an Instagram post branded in your copy with something like, "Problem: Interest rates are high and you're having trouble finding a great deal on a home." Solution: As an industry-ranked specialist, I negotiate a lower interest rate of up to 2% to help you get into the home of your dreams. (This could work with something like a seller "buy down.")

6. Testimonials

This is where you will store created cards, videos, or other content of customers giving your business a testimonial. I prefer pushing my testimonial or review requests to my client's Google My Business profile, then copying those reviews to create beautifully branded cards for social media.

7. Quote Cards

These are great ways to break up the visual drudgery of too many images. These generally consist of a quote relevant to your industry overlaid on another image.

8. Recycle

In this folder, you can store some of your best-performing content to reuse again and again! I recommend waiting about 60 days before you start recycling content, but it can help fill content gaps later on, as well as give you a breather when you need it. By recycling your best content, your audience gets the benefit of seeing it again, while you get a creativity break.

So how do you reuse content? If you posted a photo of a gorgeous white kitchen in February, you could repost that photo in April with a different caption. Whereas in February, you might have written, "Check out this home for sale" with a link to the listing or to the agent, in April, the copy could be, "3 ways to photograph a white kitchen."

A note on recycling content: recycling content can save your sanity, but only if you don't overuse it. Recycling a piece every 60–90 days is more than enough. While opinions vary, starting out, recycled content should never make up more than 20 percent of your month's posts, or your audience may tire of your content and brand.

CONTENT TYPES AND ORGANIZING YOUR FOLDERS

Once upon a time, I worked with an agency that managed funnel builds. I worked with a client who had created a PDF download for her course, "365 Social Media Content Ideas."

Inside the PDF, the 365 ideas were grouped by profession with prompts. It was color-coded and beautiful. I wanted to try it.

At the time, I was a contractor and starting up my own small agency. I asked if I could test the prompts by using the post suggestions to create content for Instagram.

For agencies and service-based businesses like mine that don't simply have a lot of images lying around, curating content can be tricky and time-consuming.

Even with the prompts, designing branded images for my Instagram to cross-post to Facebook (posting and scheduling for only two channels) took time away from other revenue-generating tasks and from my family.

I struggled. Hard. I just didn't see the point. It was a long game, and I was looking for quick wins. So, fast forward two weeks, and I had stopped posting. Sound familiar?

I know that story backward and forward. Instagram is one of the best channels for reaching new audiences organically—right now. Yet, unless your business is wheeling and dealing in images and you have access to tons of images almost every day or you just love promoting yourself on social media and taking selfies wherever you go, Instagram can be a harder nut to crack.

When I started really looking at Instagram, I knew we needed a system to make it work. I tested by creating a Dropbox folder using the folder organization hierarchy I showed you with content folders and organizing the content in each folder.

I set up and used a free kanban-style project management tool called Trello to plan the initial strategy for the month, schedule the content, assign tasks for my virtual assistant team, and then gave my VAs freedom to run the plays.

Trello became our "command center." It's easy to use and easy to implement. With a very small learning curve compared to many other project management software programs I have used, our little team was up and running.

To help you get started running your own plays, you also need to have a well-organized place where you can communicate with your team, store your strategies, and coordinate together.

⇨BUILD YOUR BUSINESS EXERCISE: STOCKING THE POND

If you start by posting two times per day to get the algorithms of Instagram and Facebook kicking in your favor, you'll need around sixty images for month one.

As real estate agents or real estate photographers, you already have access to at least thirty-six photos for each listing you've worked on. This content can be reused on your social media. In this exercise, I want you to go through your available images and start filling your folders with content for the next month.

You should only need to supply new photos for the other categories (behind the scenes, meet the team, community, and testimonials). And these photos are super easy to get.

For this exercise, estimate it will take 30 to 45 minutes to sort your images for the next month into your subfolders. Refer back to the description of each folder as needed.

WHEREFORE ART THOU CONTENT?

My first month using this strategy, I planned a month's worth of posts in Trello, only to realize I was low in a lot of the top-performing content categories—specifically BTS and Community Shots for Ben.

I started letting the VA schedule what I had and set a date with Ben and the kids. We blocked out 4 hours on a Saturday, grabbed his camera equipment, and headed downtown with a brand shot list.

I'm not a photographer, but we got a lot of great shots that we still recycle and use for social media (yes, even three years later) using just his iPhone and the shot list I printed out that morning. We also had a lot of fun! It's that easy!

⇨BUILD YOUR BUSINESS EXERCISE: FINDING AND CREATING NEW CONTENT

Looking at the subfolders where you store your images, you may find some gaps. If you don't have five to ten images in one category, spend some time filling the gaps with content.

For example, if you have a client meeting coming up that week, you could set a reminder on your calendar to get a photo with the client and take a fun photo of you with the staff or a food photo of your favorite dish.

Don't have any client dates coming up?

Grab a friend and book yourself a date! If you talk about your business, and use your business card, you can get a write off for the meal as well.

Need to grab a friend for a shot list photoshoot day? I've included a copy of the PDF of the shot list we used inside the course materials available with this book.

PROJECT HUB RECOMMENDATIONS

I mentioned earlier that in my first month, I planned an entire month's strategy in Trello. If you don't know or aren't familiar with Trello, it is a magnificently simple project management tool.

In Trello, you can add team members, add Power-Ups (productivity add-ons), and have multiple boards for organizing your projects. My team and I use Trello to plan social media posts for the month for our clients, have easy access to brand kits and brand guidelines, and have a one-stop shop for project and task-related communication. We also use it to organize other projects, like the publication and launch strategy for this book.

> **Important note:** Some social media scheduling softwares include a lot of the features of Trello: a visual planning calendar, a process checklist for scheduling posts, color-coded content category labels, and more. Other software options do not offer these features. For this reason, I recommend plan-

ning your initial 30-day strategy in Trello first to get a feel for how to plan your social media as a project.

Once you know the features you like and the features that are helpful to you, you can drop the extra step of planning in Trello and plan directly in your scheduling software of choice. I'll review a few features and benefits of some scheduling software later in this chapter.

⇨BUILD YOUR BUSINESS EXERCISE: CREATE YOUR PROJECT HUB

If you're not already using a digital project management tool for your business, like Airtable, Asana, or Trello, I recommend setting one up now to help you organize your content categories. While you can try the following strategy with something like Google Sheets, I recommend Trello. It currently has a very powerful free option. The calendar option makes viewing your content for the month a breeze. You can easily assign tasks with due dates.

To use Trello the way my team and I use it, sign up for a free account and create your first board. Your board is the project you will be working on. You can have several boards in Trello—one for each project. As this board is for managing your social media accounts and content, you may want to name it something simple, like "Social Media."

Once inside, navigate to your menu and select Power-Ups to add the Calendar feature. While you're here, go ahead and add the appropriate Power-Up for your cloud-based storage solution (Google Drive, Dropbox, etc.) where you will store your images and other content.

PSST: I've included a pre-made, plug-and-play strategy Trello board, complete with a video walkthrough on how to organize it, with the course companion for this book at SocialMediaOnAuto.com/Course.

YOUR INITIAL 30-DAY STRATEGY

With your project hub of choice created, it's now time to plan your first 30 days of content. This is your testing ground. Remember, any content you test in this period and every period after is a test. Content is always a test. Use the exercise below, along with the color-coded labels I recommend, to help you create your first 30-day strategy.

At the end of the 30 days, you can check your analytics in Flick to see which content types, posting times, captions, and hashtags resonated the best with your target audience. Don't be afraid to let this first 30-day sprint look a little messy. We're not aiming for perfection. We're aiming to discover trends so that we can systemize and automate the process.

⇨BUILD YOUR BUSINESS EXERCISE: CREATE YOUR INITIAL 30-DAY STRATEGY

In Trello, you'll create a single card for each of the six content types. After creating the card, use the Trello "label" feature to label each card for the category it will represent.

Color-coding works wonders. Select a color for each content category, one color per content folder. As you create your content cards and schedule them in your calendar, these pops of color allow you to quickly look at your content types visually to see if you have too many of one type of content or not enough of another.

At this point, I find it helpful to flip over to Calendar view, so that you can make sure you schedule a card for each day inside your 30-day calendar. Remember, each card on your calendar represents a post to your social media channels.

You already have thirty to sixty images to play with, so play. Schedule at least one piece of content per day, and vary the content. Don't schedule two of the same types of content on the same day.

For example, your Monday post may be a BTS (a post about a coffee spill that nearly fried your Mac or PC), your Tuesday post could be from the Services category (an exterior home photo), and your Wednesday post could be a MTT post (where you introduce a photographer on your staff, Suzie).

Practice attaching an image you want to post for that month to a corresponding Trello card. To attach your image, look for the Power-Up for the cloud-based storage option you chose listed on the card. Next, write a line or two of copy in the "Description" section of the card. Finally, add a "due date," which is the date you want the post to go live on your social media channels. This is the same process you will use when you train your VA to take over social media for you later.

PRO-TIP: When training your virtual assistant for the first month or two, you may want to create a checklist in each card to help them remember each step of scheduling the post. Essentially, the checklist becomes a SOP, or standard operating procedure, inside the card.

Here is an example checklist.

Ready for Copy

Use this checklist item to either remind yourself to write the copy or to indicate that you'd like your VA to write the copy.

Hashtags/Schedule

This item indicates the image and copy are complete in the card, and the card is ready for hashtags to be researched and the post to be scheduled.

Revision Requested

This checklist item is helpful if you need to request any revisions from your VA, for example, "Please swap image #3 in the carousel to this image instead."

Finalized/Ready to Post

When you have approved any changes from "Revision Requested," you can assign this task to your VA, indicating the post is ready to be scheduled.

Scheduled

Your VA can check this off to complete the card and drag it to the "Scheduled" or "Complete" column. (Periodically, you'll want to archive or delete old cards.)

This process will take more time as you're learning, but it will get faster as you go. Before you know it, you could plan a 30-day strategy in as little as 10-15 minutes. Even as you get faster, the goal is not to stay here, in planning and managing your content, but to hire someone to plan, create content, build your brand, and help you analyze statistical trends within 30 to 60 days.

Until you're ready to hire this planning process out, however, you are a social media scientist. You will be testing content, learning a new process, training yourself, and setting up a system that you can train your future VA on.

Keep the content diverse. When you're finished scheduling your content, use the Calendar Power-Up in Trello to view your visual calendar. If you discover you have too many posts in one content category in a week, you can simply drag the cards and arrange them in your visual calendar to help keep your content interesting.

CONTENT ORGANIZATION AND SCHEDULING SYSTEMS

Seven Sanity Saving Tips For Managing Social Media Effectively

Number One

For goodness' sake, don't be a slave to social media. Schedule it and run it. Then, you can go back and look at the numbers later to see if your experiment worked.

Number Two

If you want to post live streams, reels, or other videos, schedule them. Can you do it on the fly? Yes. But you don't have to.

Number Three

Your posted content is only as good as the material you give yourself and your VA to work with. Using the Recycled Content folder will give you room, but make sure that you keep your content folders stocked. Take photos and upload them to your content folders as you take them to create a stockpile for later.

Number Four

Social media is organic. Organic takes time. Can you skyrocket an account in 30 days with fresh content and by staying tuned in 24/7? Yep. But who in the world has that kind of time? Be prepared for the tradeoff. Slow and steady will win the race.

Number Five

Consistency is key. You can sprint for thirty days and create a ton of content, and then easily burn out. (I did.) Or you can work to grow your social accounts, followers, clicks to your website, and leads—one month at a time—all while you run your business and maintain your life.

Number Six

Work toward long-term, sustainable account growth, month over month, to grow website traffic, generate leads, and own your market.

Number Seven

Make sure your website pages are conversion-optimized. A simple, basic design is preferred. There's no need for fancy, flashy websites. People just want something they can navigate in three seconds or less.

If you're driving your social media traffic to a website that doesn't convert traffic into leads, you're wasting your time and your prospects' time.

SOCIAL MEDIA SCHEDULING PLATFORMS AND SOFTWARES

There are many services and programs that you can use for scheduling your content. Here are a few I like.

Meta Business Suite Content Planner

This is the best social media scheduler that I've found so far for optimizing Instagram reach. Formerly called Creator Studio, this planner built and offered by Meta offers a native platform option for scheduling Facebook and Instagram posts, stories, and reels.

Because Meta owns both channels, Facebook and Instagram, you'll find a lot of tools inside for optimizing reach and engagement. That said, my team and I are constantly testing new software for increased results, and there are a handful of paid scheduling software options out there now that are working hard and fast to offer the full suite of services that this platform offers for Facebook and Instagram—for free.

You can schedule Instagram and Facebook posts seamlessly, with alt text and all the bells and whistles included. It only works for Facebook and Instagram, meaning you need a different service for scheduling LinkedIn and Google My Business, but the features are worth it.

Meta Business Suite also gives you a calendar view so that you can see what times your content is scheduled for, as well as some very basic analytics.

You can view post metrics in the Insights portion of Meta Business Suite as well. Meta is currently bringing over additional content and analytics from its former software, Creator Studio, as it merges Facebook Business Suite and Creator Studio products.

An additional (and possibly simpler) place to look at your post metrics is inside your Page's professional dashboard. To access these insights on desktop, go to your business page profile on Facebook, then scroll down the left-side menu to navigate to "Insights."

All-In-One Scheduling Softwares:

If you want an easy solution to schedule all your content in one place and are okay with losing a little reach for the sake of convenience, there are a few services you can try. Pricing is accurate as of the publication of this book.

Here are a few of my favorite programs and tools:

Loomly

$35 per month for the base account. A discount is available with a yearly plan.

You can use Loomly to schedule posts to Facebook, Instagram, Twitter, Pinterest, LinkedIn, and Google My Business. It also offers a host of other sweet features, including post ideas and optimization tips.

Sprout Social

$448 per month for a standard account with two users.

You can use Sprout Social to schedule posts for Facebook, Instagram, LinkedIn, Twitter, Pinterest, Google My Business, and YouTube.

Sprout Social pricier than other options as it's geared more toward agencies.

OneUpApp.io

$24 per month, unlimited team members

OneUp can schedule Facebook, Instagram, Google My Business, Twitter, LinkedIn, Pinterest, and TikTok.

Use the calendar view to get a view of your posts, like you would with Planable and Trello.

OneUp is easy to use and get started with.

Planable

$52 per month with two users and ten category labels to help organize your content (as in Trello).

Planable can schedule posts to Facebook, Instagram, LinkedIn, Twitter, Google My Business, and TikTok.

Planable's drag-and-drop schedule planner may eliminate the need to plan content in Trello, but some still prefer the functionality of Trello over Planable for strategy planning. If you choose to use Planable, you may still want a place, even a Google Drive folder, to store VA training and other content.

Planable allows you to easily add users (like your virtual assistant) and set up pre-approval workflows for a fee.

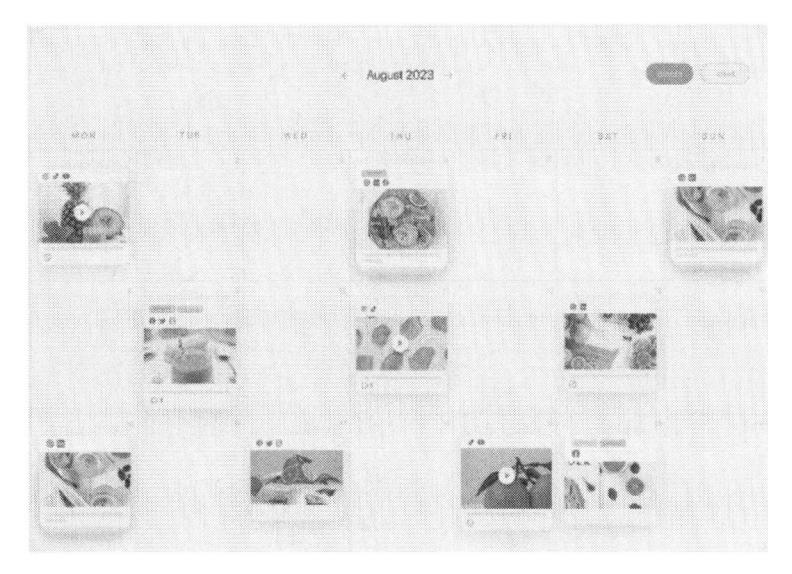

Planable Visual Calendar View

⇨ BUILD YOUR BUSINESS EXERCISE: CHOOSING THE BEST SCHEDULING SOFTWARE

Let's get real here.

There are A LOT more services that you can try. I suggested the services above because they allow you to schedule your Google My Business posts as well. But it's time to dive in.

So pick one and play with it for a few days. Schedule a few days' worth of content on it. See what you think. Then try another one.

Find one service that makes the user experience so easy and simple that you can easily explain it to your VA later on with a simple video or two.

When you've landed on your software of choice, go ahead and schedule your first month of content. You've already planned your initial strategy in Trello, so if you would like, you can try a few different scheduling softwares during their trial periods—without losing all the hard work you did in the planning phase. Choose a software option, schedule a week's worth of content during a trial period, and see how you like the user interface.

If the idea of testing different software gives you a headache, make it easy on yourself and simply commit to one and run with it. Remember, this decision isn't set in stone. Find one that works for you and your business now, so you don't put off getting started.

📷 FOCUS POINTS

We covered a lot in this chapter. Here's a quick recap of what you learned and the exercises you should have completed before moving on to the next chapter, Social Media Copywriting!

In this chapter, you learned how much content you really need, overcame any resistance you may have previously held about social media, and discovered what types of content sell—building know, like, and trust for you.

You also:

- set up your content folders—a strategy that helps in the beginning phases as you learn which types of content your audience enjoys the most from you;

- stocked the pond by filling your content folders with the right types of content to get your first thirty days off to a great start;
- learned quick tips for finding and creating new content for any folders where there wasn't enough content to start with;
- created your project hub or team dashboard—the project management tool you used to create your initial social media strategy;
- created the post strategy for your first thirty days;
- and you scheduled at least one post per day for the next thirty days, making sure to vary the types of content from your folder system to create content diversity in your feed.

EIGHT
WHAT TO WRITE?

Your content is organized. Your initial 30-day strategy plan is set in Trello (or another project hub). You have your starter hashtags organized in collections in Flick. You've connected Flick to your Instagram account for monitoring and maintenance. You've chosen a social media scheduling platform. Now, what in the world do you write for the copy of each post?

In the first thirty days, maybe sixty, I wrote all the copy for Ben. I was still getting a feel for my virtual assistant's grasp of American English and local slang terms used in social media copy.

As I had some previous copywriting training, I was able to punch out a week's worth of copy, or enough for fourteen posts, in about half an hour.

However, I didn't want to be tied to this. I realized, as my company grew and I took on more clients, that me writing all the copy would be a bottleneck to growth.

I tested a few systems and found one that worked for my team and me. Soon, I was able to hand off copywriting to my team.

They now manage short copy successfully for all our accounts, which, for most social media posts, is all you need.

Ad copy can perform better with long copy, but in our tests, short copy that was skimmable and delivered the message worked well for organic traffic and account growth objectives, while allowing the Virtual Assistant to feel confident enough to post without coming to you with copywriting questions.

In this chapter, you'll learn a few ways you can overcome your copywriting resistance using little hacks that I will teach you. I encourage you to try them all, one at a time, until you find a system that works for you.

SOCIAL MEDIA COPYWRITING CHEATS FOR FAST, EFFECTIVE COPY

It's true that photos tell stories. Bad photos. Great photos. Grainy photos. Composed photos. Each photo is a reflection of the world at that time through the eye of the person who captured it.

We, as humans, learn best and connect most through stories.

It's why every good TedEx speaker starts out with a personal story—to get your attention. If they went right into what they wanted to teach you, you'd tune them out.

Photos grab attention.

Story sells.

SOCIAL MEDIA STORYTELLING

Weaving storytelling into your posts will increase your engagement and reach. Your audience wants to know about the person (or people) behind the brand.

Here are a few ways to use storytelling in your copywriting. After reviewing them, use the copywriting hacks that follow to write the copy for your scheduled posts.

Positioning Your Brand Through Problem/Solution Posts

The fifty problems and solutions you listed earlier can be turned into visual images or shortened to fit onto an Instagram square or portrait post. There are two easy ways to play with this format.

Visual Image and Long Copy

Try taking a photo that represents the problem your customers are facing. In the copy, empathize with the pain your customers are experiencing. Let them know, you have felt it also. Then, position your solution as the answer to the problem. You can reveal yourself or your service as the answer to their problem in the copy itself.

Multiple Images And Copy Tease

Another way to showcase Problem/Solution posts is to create a separate image card showing the solution. When you post a multiple-image post on Instagram, users must tap or scroll to see the next image, which increases your engagement score. You can address their problem with shorter copy, then tease the solution to their problem in the post with something like "See photo #2 for the solution!"

Video Summary

If you decide to post videos, summarize what your audience will learn with simple bullet points in the copy above or below the video. Many people watch videos. Many people skim videos. Many people watch the first three seconds of a video, then leave. By summarizing what your audience will learn from watching your video, you give them an incentive to watch it to the end.

Unexpected Change

The most popular TV and book series use this technique often to keep audiences interested. Also referred to as a "plot twist," unexpected changes can be teased for days or weeks before the final reveal. Think of some of your favorite products or services. Have you ever seen posts teasing a new product or new solution coming soon? These posts stack well after a few thoughtfully placed Problem/Solution style posts that acknowledge and agitate the problem in your audience's mind.

Shareable Content

As you're considering what to write about, remember that while the copy should address the image, it doesn't have to match the image.

People share content on social media that informs, excites them, makes them laugh, or even helps communicate an aspect of their identity—something that they care about.

Adding a bit of humor or human relatability to your posts can help them get shared more often. This is one of the reasons I love quote cards. They are an easy way to create shareable content. Finding quotes from books you're reading, quotes from philosophers, song lyrics, quotes from comedians, or even your favorite movie can help you create more universal content that your audience will be willing to share. If you can quote yourself, even better!

Emotional Copy

This may be a bit harder for your VA to write for you unless they are fluent in both English and the culture of your country or audience.

When sharing emotional content—congratulating a team member, expressing thanks, sharing a sad moment or loss, sharing a goal—it's important to write in your brand voice and add just enough emotion to connect with the audience without overwhelming them or making them feel isolated from you.

COPYWRITING HACKS FOR SOCIAL MEDIA

Using Other People's Words (a.k.a. The Quote Post)

Want an easy win? Do you have a great photo of a sunset over a lake next to a house you shot?

Google: "Sunset quotes." Then, copy and paste the quote, making sure to attribute the original speaker or author.

Write a few short sentences about what the quote means to you and your company. Write a sentence or two about the effect that quote had on you the moment you read it. You may even choose to tie this to an upcoming event at your company or some recent news you've wanted to share.

Look through your hashtags, using the Local Thirds Strategy you learned in Chapter Four. Choose your 27–30 hashtags.

Schedule the post for Instagram, copying the post to all other platforms. Delete the hashtags from your Facebook, LinkedIn, Google My Business, and YouTube posts.

Done.

Artificial Intelligence Copy

Jasper.AI

Wouldn't it be great if a robot could write the copy for you? They can. I'm a big fan of Jasper. You can get a free trial at bit.ly/jasperSMOAStrial.

Using the templates available inside Jasper, describe your photo and then let Jasper write it for you. Jasper will offer you several options. Choose the one that works best for your post. A great feature that comes with Jasper is the ability to change the tone or voice of your post. You could tell Jasper to write you a 300-character funny description of a photo of clown shoes or a 300-character nostalgic, lonely description of a photo of clown shoes, and it can do both and a lot more.

ChatGPT

Another tool that just exploded on the scene in November 2022 is ChatGPT. ChatGPT 4.0 was recently released, and while research and development is still being explored, one 5-10 minute dive down the YouTube rabbit hole on this API will astound you.

Built-In AI Copywriting Tool

Many social media scheduling software options now have AI tools built right in. These are great time-savers for those who need a lot of copy, really fast.

Pocket Copy Deck

Do you ever wish you had a deck of cards you could just pull out on the go, like a deck of cards? You can!

Copywriting templates are a bit like old-school Mad Libs. You find a few that you're drawn to, then copy those and save them in an online, cloud-based application.

This can be a Google Doc or a card in your Trello project management system.

Here are a few copy templates, along with some examples of how one might fill them in for their business.

With this method, it is possible to sit down and crank out fifty of these in under half an hour over coffee. I recommend having these written out in a Google Drive doc or Trello card to copy and paste as needed, rotating them with different photos.

How can [YOUR AUDIENCE] do [ACTION] better with [YOUR PRODUCT/SERVICE]?

How busy moms with multiple kids in Greenville are keeping their homes decluttered during home showings using this 5-minute tidying tip.

How Greenville realtors are flipping houses and raking in cash with multiple listings, using my 24-hour professional photography turnaround service.

[INSERT PROBLEM]? We've got your solution.

Getting "Under Asking" bids? I've got your solution.

Do [INSERT TASK] better.

Sell your house faster.

Faster than your neighbor.

Faster than the house that won the "best lawn" award last year.

Here's how.

Copy/Paste from your MLS listing

This may be the simplest copy hack, but you can simply reuse what you already wrote for a property listing. Copy and paste the MLS listing description you wrote for a recent home or commercial property listing. Modify the copy a bit, taking into account formatting for social media and character count limitations. Then, post it. It's as easy as that.

⇨ BUILD YOUR BUSINESS: COPYWRITING FOR THE REST OF US

Before moving on to the next section, choose two strategies from this section you want to test for the next 30 days.

SEO SLEEPER STRATEGY: HIDING KEYWORDS IN PLAIN SIGHT

Want to learn my super sneaky, three-second trick for ranking images on Google? It's alt text.

> "Also called alt tags and alt descriptions, alt text is the written copy that appears in place of an image on a webpage if the image fails to load on a user's screen. This text helps screen-reading tools describe images to visually impaired readers and allows search engines to better crawl and rank your website." -Hubspot

When I first started dabbling in content creation and internet marketing in 2008, I created and ran a blog for a local natural/holistic pet food company in town.

Using an old service, Google Blogger, I decided to write articles to share in an email newsletter to our customers. The articles contained all the pet food "nerd" knowledge I had acquired. Nothing big. Nothing I thought of as groundbreaking. I didn't know much about keywords or SEO at the time. I simply knew I wanted to help.

I discovered, in my "playing around," that the images I inserted into the blog to help people better understand the content had an empty text field that I could fill in with words when I went to upload the photo to the blog post. I started using that text field to "describe" the image as if I were explaining it to someone who was visually impaired. Usually, this involves tying in a keyword or two.

For example:

"Dog on side panting in pain suffering acute pancreatitis"

"Prescription diet used to treat acute pancreatitis in dogs"

"Dog in pain after Thanksgiving turkey and gravy"

You get the idea. While I didn't know enough about keywords yet to rank the blog text itself, the posts began to rank on Google magically—simply based on the alt text I had used to describe the images.

That year and for three years after, we continued to gain rank on Google for some very basic blog posts, maybe 800 words long and written by a newbie. Of those 23 posts, five did very well and drove over 65 percent of new site traffic to our website for three consecutive years. We didn't run ads, buy media, send mailers, or do networking. With just a few words written to describe an image on a page that had great information, we were getting noticed.

The articles drove traffic. The traffic turned into sales. We gained traction over our competition simply by using search terms that they were sleeping on in the "alt text" field. This is why I call the "alt text" field my Sleeper Strategy. An extra ten seconds can give your account more reach and help your images appear in Google Search Results for your business or service later.

You can also use this strategy on your social media platforms.

Images posted on Instagram, Facebook, and LinkedIn (even Pinterest and Twitter) all allow you to use alt text to describe the image you are about to post—so you might as well get the "free" SEO traffic as you're posting your images.

Not all scheduling softwares provide a place to include alt text on your images, so you'll need to decide if this strategy works for you when weighing your scheduling software options.

Step 1: Name the Image

Name the image as if you were describing it to a visually impaired person. You can see in the example below that I named this file "home with pool for sale Greenville, SC—Ben Ivins Media."

Now, is this the best description? Not necessarily.

I could also have named this photo:

123 Main Street Home for Sale with Pool in Greenville, SC

Or

home with pool for sale Real estate photography Greenville, SC

Or

Home for sale with pool 123 Main Street Greenville SC—Ben Ivins Media Real Estate Photography

The trick with alt text is to mix up the copy a bit. Don't "keyword stuff" your images so that your posts get flagged by search engines. Write a description that is helpful and authentic to search engines and to anyone who is visually impaired. Then, maybe in every fourth or fifth post, you can tag yourself as the photographer or the real estate agency responsible for the photo.

Step 2: Copy the File Name for Your Alt Text

When you go to schedule the post, use the file name as your alt text.

Following the same example, the alt text field would look like this:

Save the image, add your copy, tag yourself in the Instagram post, and you're good to go.

For maximum conversions using the Sleeper Strategy:

> Check your strategy monthly to see how many people are finding your images and clicking through to your social media profiles from the image search.

> Make sure your social media profiles make it easy for people to get to your website quickly. There should only be two clicks —one on your image to your social media profile, then one from your social media profile to your website.

Final Sleeper Strategy Tips

As you schedule your content, review your keywords from your research phase. Make sure to include them, when and where appropriate, in your photo and video posts.

Property addresses are great alt-text properties to include.

Remember, do not overuse one keyword phrase or a few keyword phrases within a short period of time to try to game Google and search engines. They are smarter than you know.

FOCUS POINTS

This chapter was all about copy hacks and the Sleeper Strategy. In this chapter, we covered:

- five examples of storytelling through social media content copywriting;
- an easy starter post for anyone looking to fill content gaps (a.k.a. the quote post);

- A.I. copywriting cheats;
- an introduction to copywriting mad-libs;
- and I gave you a simple strategy you can use to gain rank from Google image searches.

Before you move on to Chapter 8, choose at least two of the copy hacks in this chapter and use them to write captions for one to two weeks' worth of posts. You can write your captions directly in the "Description" field inside the Trello card for that post.

NINE
UNDERSTANDING REPORTS AND ANALYZING YOUR DATA

It's amazing, as a perfectionist and professional, how much wanting everything to be perfect has held me back from starting things.

Allowing yourself the freedom to fail as well as the freedom to learn is the key to a successful business.

The faster you fail, the faster you learn, and the faster you win.

In this chapter, you'll learn about realistic goal setting for your first thirty to sixty days and a bit about how to read the numbers to see if you're going in the right direction.

For Instagram growth metrics, I rely on using the analytics dashboard found in Flick as my primary source of data, supplementing with information from Instagram in Meta Business Suite, Instagram business account growth metrics, and other various spaces.

The examples I show in this chapter will be based on using Flick, as that is my current tool of preference.

The point is: choose one analytics dashboard and get started.

WHEN TO CHECK

If you've gone through and scheduled your first week of content, you may be very tempted to check the engagement on your posts every hour, every two hours, or maybe even multiple times a day.

This is the road to "Crazy Town" for many.

Many will drop off, stop posting, and abandon social media as a viable strategy if they don't see lottery ticket-style "instant wins" within a three-to-five day window.

Don't do it.

If you *need* to peek at your numbers, discipline yourself to check your stats once every two to three days.

Instead of looking at how many "hearts" you got on your posts in the feed, look at the Flick dashboard and look for growth.

If you see that your engagement rate is up 20 percent or 200 percent, you're on the right track.

Here are the numbers to watch:

> **Reach and Impressions**
>
> These numbers tell you how many times your content has been seen.
>
> **Follower Growth**
>
> This tells you how many new followers you gained within the time period or lookback window.

Engagement Score

This number is a calculated score measuring how much people like your content.

Profile Visits

This number shows how many times people left the feed to visit your social media profile or social media page.

Website Clicks

This is the number of times people clicked on your profile link to visit your website.

Email

Very simply, this is the number of times people clicked to email you from your social channel.

Phone Calls

This number shows the number of times people clicked on a button on one of your channels to call you.

Now, remember our sales funnel?

THE FUNNEL FRAMEWORK

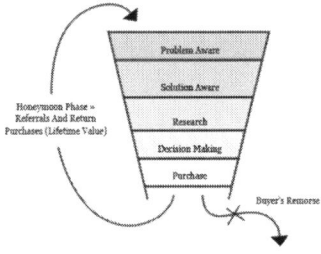

Honeymoon Phase = Referrals And Return Purchases (Lifetime Value)

- Problem Aware
- Solution Aware
- Research
- Decision Making
- Purchase

Buyer's Remorse

We're trying to build reach, impressions, followers, and engagement to get them into your funnel. From there, we want to move them down your funnel into the research and decision-making phases by having them click on your profile, visit your website, and/or contact you.

In Flick, those statistics will look like this:

Reach and Impressions

The first step in engaging with your audience is reaching and impressing them with information about your brand, the services you offer, and the problems you can solve for them.

Followers

As your audience becomes more interested in your brand, they may start following you, indicating that they are intrigued by your message and how you can help them solve their problems.

Engagement

Engagement is the next step in building a relationship with your audience and represents their emotional buy-in to your message. Positive engagement, such as likes and affirmative comments, shows that they are interested in learning more about your product or service.

Profile Visits

Visiting your profile is a crucial step in building a relationship with your audience and helps establish the "know, like, and trust" factor.

Website Clicks

When someone clicks on your website, they are actively searching for a solution and are in the consideration phase, considering whether you could be the one to help solve their problem.

Email or Phone

Contact methods, such as email or phone, provide your audience with an opportunity to learn more about your brand and services, get pricing information, and clear up any misunderstandings or objections they may have.

EXPECTATIONS AND REFLECTION

In the first few days, you may only see a few likes and maybe a comment or two. That's okay. Just like with any new initiative, building something new takes a little time. Take a step back and look at the data after a week.

Which posts got the most comments? Which images? Which copy? Which hashtags? Which days and times of day were the best for engagement?

Make a note somewhere—a journal, a Google Doc, an Excel spreadsheet, or better yet, a card in your Project Hub—of the things you see.

Did a photo of you with cake on your face at a coworker's birthday celebration get the most likes? Not surprising. People like photos of people, photos of behind-the-scenes action, photos of people in real life, and photos of funny things. You combined four elements in a single post there. Try another photo with a similar element or two.

Maybe it's just a photo of you smiling at your favorite cafe while you work, which would fulfill two things for the strategy: a photo of a face and a look behind the scenes.

Did three of your posts all contain similar hashtags? Did they do well? What was the same? What's different? Did they perform poorly?

Did posts on Monday do better than posts on Thursday? Why? Was the content the same or different?

You won't have the answers to all of these questions in one week. Truly, one week of data is simply not enough to make real decisions off of. I prefer to work in sixty-to-ninety day windows to look for definitive patterns, but a week's worth of data is enough to make a few small inferences.

After you've posted your first month of content, you should be fairly familiar with:

- which content pieces your audience seems to enjoy;
- which types of content perform best on which platform;
- the best posting schedule for you for ROI and work-life balance;
- how to navigate your different systems and software;
- and how to read basic account reports to look for patterns or opportunities for growth.

TRAINING YOUR VIRTUAL ASSISTANT

After your first thirty days of successfully scheduled content and analysis, you could begin to record videos of your set-up and strategy for your future virtual assistant. These videos will be helpful training tools that you can record using a screen recording software of your choice, explaining each step as you create and schedule your month-two content.

I recommend saving and organizing your videos in sequential order, from start to finish, in a filing system in DropBox or Google Drive so that they can be easily accessed by your future hire.

Then you can simply create and assign tasks in Trello (or your project hub) for things like "Watch videos 1—3 and comment with any questions" or "Schedule three posts using what you learned from videos 4—6".

If you're using one of the other social media scheduling systems with workflow capabilities, you can test that there, as well.

As you get more comfortable with your social media strategy and the posts your virtual assistant makes for you, you should be able to shift away from working on social media every day. It is realistic to expect to spend one hour per month reading and interpreting your reports and one hour per month on VA management.

You now have set up your Social Media On Auto strategy to run almost completely automatically for you, managed for as little as two hours a month.

FOCUS POINTS

After reading this chapter, you should know and be familiar with:

- when to check your reports in Flick and other report sources such as Facebook Professional Dashboard, Meta Business Suite/Creator Studio, YouTube Studio, and LinkedIn;
- what metrics to look at and what kind of growth to expect during your first thirty days of posting;
- and how to record and organize training videos for your virtual assistant hire as you schedule your month-two content.

TEN
GOAL SETTING & HIRING YOUR VIRTUAL ASSISTANT

PLANNING FOR SUCCESS

When you are setting your goals for your next month or two of business, keep in mind that your goals should be S.M.A.R.T. goals.

When sharing these goals with your VA, it can help to include them in the conversation.

I love asking my virtual assistants for their opinions. I like doing this because

1. I'm human and sometimes other people have better ideas than me, and
2. it allows me to see their level of strategic understanding of what we're doing.

Make your goals reasonable, with a little dash of challenge, so that you can celebrate the win! Here are a couple of S.M.A.R.T. goals you can try as you get started:

- increase follower growth by X percent;
- increase reach by X percent;
- increase website clicks by X percent;
- and increase the engagement rate by X percent.

If your first month's goal is to post 45 pieces of content and grow your account by 30 followers, that's great!

Next month, you'll have some data to work with, and you can set percentage-based growth goals. If you don't hit your goals, remember: don't bash your virtual assistant. They are here to help you grow your business. Try analyzing your reports to see what was missed. How can you both improve?

HIRING YOUR VIRTUAL ASSISTANT

There are hundreds of places to find your perfect virtual assistant. Sometimes, you'll get the right hire the first time. But, like hiring people for any position, often hiring the person to do an amazing job at scheduling your social media may require a few hires to find the person who is the best fit.

There are multiple places you can post job descriptions for your hiring process, including Upwork and OnlineJobs.ph. Some of these platforms require paying a fee to join, while others are free to join but you pay to reply to interested applicants. You may also know someone local who can manage social media for you.

Here are a few tips and strategies to help you navigate the hiring process.

Be Professional

Have your systems set up and your training videos completed before attempting to hire. A professional assistant wants to be hired by a professional. While systems change as we learn and grow, and your playbooks should be constantly updated to reflect this, having a good starter protocol will allow clear communication and set clear expectations for your virtual assistant up front.

Learning a new system or job can be stressful. Make it easy for them so that they can do amazing work for you. Remember, they are few and far between who enjoy working for the "hot mess" boss person. Set your systems and your person up to excel.

Writing Your Job Description

When you're ready to create your job post, your headline for the post should include the type of work needed, for example, "Social Media Virtual Assistant." Make sure that you address and detail the scope of work clearly in the job description section.

An example might be, "Tasks include: monthly social media strategy review; writing social media copy; photo editing and manipulation to create eye-catching content for multiple channels; and bulk scheduling of social media posts a minimum of two weeks in advance. You'll coordinate weekly with the project owner until fully trained for 15-minute weekly check-in sessions."

You'll also want to list any hard or soft skills you need from your VA. These can be things like native or proficient English speakers, available hours, and software you would like them to be proficient with before starting with you.

While I believe most of the software I've covered in this book is easy to learn, it is fantastic if you hire someone who is already familiar with the software that you use, so they simply have to learn your system. This cuts down on their stress level, and oftentimes, they may know software secrets to make things easier and better for you—that even you didn't know!

Code Words

Pro-Tip: In your job description, include a code word in the middle or toward the bottom to ensure the person applying has read your full post. You can say things like, "Reply with the word banana in your subject line to be considered." As silly as this sounds, you'll be surprised at how many replies you get from people who don't even take time to read your job posting fully. This can carry over into their future work for you, such as skipping steps in processes, etc. You don't want that.

Creating Test Jobs

If you've found a person you would like to consider for the position, create a test job for them. This could be as simple as, "Watch these videos and schedule two posts following the strategy laid out for you. After scheduling, reply with any questions you have," or even, "Create an engaging Instagram reel using these three video clips and this image, with three sentences of copy that would engage a realtor audience."

Make sure you pay for the test job, as you can use this in your social media that month.

Communication and Paying Your Virtual Assistant

I prefer to keep communication with my assistants in the project hub, or Trello, to begin with. You may also find quick messaging solutions that work well for questions here and there.

As your virtual assistant is a real person with their own life, family, and friends, make sure you don't bother them in their off hours. Set times when it is appropriate to correspond or message each other. Let them know they can reply during their work hours.

For payment, you'll need to find a solution that works well for you. Many business owners use PayPal Business or have their virtual assistants send them an invoice to pay.

Track your payments in your accounting or bookkeeping software, as these will be tax write-offs later.

THREE PATHS OF IMPLEMENTATION

I realize that for many people, taking the time to set up systems is overwhelming when you feel you already have no time at all.

There are three paths that you can implement to get things moving—however you do that best.

D.I.Y.—Do It Yourself

Do you feel like you have a solid grasp on the concepts in this book? Are you comfortable with a few minutes in Google to teach yourself the different steps of setting up the technology and overcoming any small obstacles you hit along the way?

I wrote this book for you. You can implement this book as is with little more than some search engine help.

And while what the user interface looks like when you try to connect Facebook to a scheduling service may change, the basic strategy is the same:

- post your content;
- reuse your content;
- set up a system that works for you;
- and then train a VA to do it for you.

I've given you the systems and software that I've found most efficient and that have worked for me. But software changes all the time.

If you have the grit, the gumption, and the patience to set this up for yourself, you will have your effective *Social Media on Auto* system set up in as little as thirty to sixty days.

Social Media On Auto Course Access

Need a helpful boost?

If you would prefer to watch someone set up, run the programs, and schedule the content while watching over their shoulder, the next option is for you.

In my video course, I walk you through each chapter with setup tips and tricks that I've learned from over thirteen years in digital marketing.

I don't believe in front-loading with a lot of fluff, so you'll find the videos to be action-oriented—short, sweet, and to the point. You can pause, rewind, fast-forward, or watch at double speed. (I call this "chipmunk speed," and it definitely works.)

In places where a printable worksheet will help you brainstorm ideas or move through the course faster, I've created those for you.

Course videos are updated as user interfaces change, along with new tips and tricks I learn along the way.

You could easily take this course, along with reading the book, set your *Social Media on Auto* systems up in as little as one week, and be ready to hire your VA in thirty to forty-five days.

D.F.Y.—Done For You

"But can't you just do it for me?"

If you need a little more help and you:

- want someone experienced to set up your tailored strategy and systems;
- want a team staying on top of the latest trends and upcoming changes;
- want a trained analyst to run monthly reports and review them for you;
- and want a team working each week to make your social media a success...

schedule a call with me or a member of my team to see if our done for you options would be a great fit for your business.

You can schedule a call with a member of my team at SocialMediaOnAuto.com/Schedule to learn more.

FINAL THOUGHTS

My hope and prayer is that you have found this book incredibly useful. If you have, please don't put it on the shelf—implement it! I would love to know how reading and applying this book has made a difference in your business and in your life.

Please leave a review, following the steps in Chapter 6: Helping Others, and reach out to me with any questions you may have.

You can reach me by email at hello@socialmediaonauto.com.

Cheers!

—Delicia—

BONUS CHAPTER: MARKETING FOR BUSINESS GROWTH 101

TERMS AND CONCEPTS YOU'LL LEARN THIS CHAPTER

- Reach
- Impressions
- Customer Journey
- Reticular Activating System (RAS)
- Touchpoints
- Recency
- Engagement Score
- The Law of Diminishing Returns
- My Introduction to Marketing

Early on, I knew I loved business. My dad owns his own business, a plumbing company, and as early as I can remember, I was at his office, doing "paperwork" and learning the computer. (Which, at 5 years old in the late 80s, basically consisted of drawing on legal pads, coloring with highlighters, and playing Wheel of Fortune on a floppy disk using DOS COMMAND://RUN to boot up the game.)

I would spend summers going to job sites with him, where I played "King of the Mountain" with my little sister, racing up giant mountains of dirt pushed up days earlier by an excavator. I had my own company t-shirt that read, "Ben's Plumbing Little Helper." He took me on supply runs, where I met the managers and owners of supply stores, and to company lunches and Christmas parties with people in the industry.

I was always listening and watching. And Dad was always ready to teach me something. He told me, "A lot of people are nervous around office people—the people that handle the paychecks and the money. They feel inferior to them. I don't want that for you. I want you to be comfortable here." I learned how to invoice, how to schedule employees, how to price jobs, and how to present myself professionally on the phone to take messages for him at a young age. I sat in on business meetings and employee hiring rounds.

After high school, I decided to go into business management. A year into that program (while simultaneously running my dad's office), I learned that I did not enjoy managing the office as much as I thought I would. The day-to-day drum of moving papers from one stack to another was mind-numbing for me, and my whole body railed against it.

I shifted my focus and my degree to marketing. I was instantly in love. Marketing mixed all the classes I adored in high school: psychology, economics, probability and statistics, English, and art.

The lessons from my dad weren't lost in marketing. I learned from him how to run a business ethically by only selling people products or services they really needed and not swindling them to make a fast dollar. In marketing, I could showcase products through testimonials and case studies, highlighting the stories of people whose lives changed because of a product or service. Some services and products really do change people's lives, and I wanted to help more people live better lives. This was my way.

I took a few semesters, working toward my Associate's Degree, before taking time off to travel, fall in love, get married, and travel for three more years. When I looped back to finish my degree, the online marketing landscape had changed. Thankfully, even during my travels, I kept up with it because it was my passion.

Previously something only large businesses could invest in, online marketing was becoming a legitimate mainstream avenue for small businesses. I realized that I couldn't learn what I needed while sitting in a classroom. I had to learn it through online courses, videos, and experience. However, I had a solid jumping-off point to start from. My introductory marketing classes and my awesome marketing professor, Mr. Marty Flynn, had taught me the building blocks of marketing psychology. Now, paired with new online strategies and technology tools, I was ready to fly.

THE SCIENCE OF MARKETING

I remember chatting with a friend of mine, Steve, at the Commerce Club one morning. "Every business owner you meet just wants to sell their gadgets," Steve said with a smile. "No one really wants to do all the marketing, invoicing, admin work, and other stuff that goes with it." I one hundred percent agree.

Which is why, once you understand what marketing is and how it functions in your business, you can automate it—well, as much of it as you can—so that you can get back to focusing on what you love: making and selling your products or services.

The purpose of marketing is simple: to drive traffic and leads to your business and help convert those leads into paying customers.

It has a simple purpose but a seemingly complex design. Marketing involves multiple touchpoints, various strategies, testing, learning, and testing again. Ever wonder why marketing is listed as a science major? A good marketer follows the scientific method for making marketing drive sales. But that's another book entirely.

What you need to know for now is that marketing is an essential part of creating and running a sustainable business. It's how you get new customers. And to that end, learning a few marketing terms can help you think differently about how you market your business. Words have power. The following words can be used to help you focus your lens, so to speak, as you zoom in on the task at hand while automating your social media marketing.

GLOSSARY OF TERMS

There are a few ideas and key terms that you'll need to understand to fully dive into building your *Social Media on Auto* machine. I'll give you definitions here, as these terms are used throughout the book. If you ever get confused, you can always flip back to this section to review the term.

Reach

Reach, or market reach, is the estimated number of people who will see (or hear) a specific marketing or advertising campaign. If you are talking to someone selling radio ads, they might say they have a reach of 500,000 listeners during the prime time your ad will air, meaning, according to their data, roughly

500,000 people will be tuned into their radio station at that particular time.

In online marketing, the definition is the same. Reach is the number of people that your posts "reaches" during the time the post went live, plus any additional reach gained from your audience sharing your post later. Reach, in social media and online advertising, means the total number of people that will see your post or your ad.

Reach is measured in unique individuals, so a reach of 2,000 means a reach of two thousand different people. The higher the reach, the more people have seen your content.

Impressions

Impressions tie into the marketing principle of frequency, which essentially means that the more times people see your content and have an emotional response to it, the more likely they are to remember your name and call you when they have a problem.

Impressions represent the number of times your content was seen or displayed, whether it was clicked on, engaged with, commented on, or not. The higher the impressions, the more your content was seen by the same people.

If you are dealing with paid advertising, another term you should be aware of is "Frequency Cap," which is the maximum number of times your ad will be seen by one person within a time period. This is sometimes displayed as a fraction or ratio, for example, 2/24. If your frequency cap is set to two, your ad may be seen a total of two times per user within a 24-hour period.

Customer Journey

This term describes the journey a prospective customer takes before doing business with your company. This is usually described in stages.

Unaware

The prospective customer is unaware they have a problem.

Problem Aware

They realize they have a problem.

Research

They actively search for a solution to their problem.

Consideration

They consider all the options available to help them solve the problem.

Decision-Making

They finalize their decision and commit to a solution.

Evaluation

They evaluate or review their decision as well as the results they achieved.

Buyer's remorse happens when someone has a bad experience or makes a bad purchasing decision during the evaluation phase. This is when someone is most likely to leave a negative review or ask for a refund.

If you've heard the term honeymoon period or honeymoon phase, this is when a customer has had success with a product or service and is feeling elated about making that decision. This is the best time to ask for a review or a referral for more business.

Reticular Activating System

The Reticular Activating System (RAS) is a part of the brain located near the top of the spinal column. All of your senses, except smell, are wired directly to this bundle of neurons. The RAS filters out information it perceives as "unnecessary", acting as the gatekeeper of information that is allowed into the conscious mind. In an age of information overload and advertising onslaught, the RAS stays quite busy.

It also regulates behavioral arousal and motivation. The RAS's main function is to streamline information, giving you just the information you need in that moment to help you survive. It accomplishes this by automating as much of your behavior as possible, which can be helpful in some ways but detrimental in others. (Hence one reason changing behavioral patterns can be difficult—they're automated and programmed by the RAS.)

Historically, as a survival mechanism, the RAS helped humans stay alive by developing pattern recognition. For example, if Caveman Sam ate a handful of red berries and then got dysentery and died, Caveman Chuck would be very wary of any red berries, no matter how dissimilar in shape to Sam's berries, for quite some time.

When Jane was out in the field gathering sticks for the fire with little Ralph and Maria clamoring about loudly behind, the RAS kicked in to allow Jane to focus in on the sound of a twig breaking in the bush, shutting out all other sounds and information, so that Jane could be alerted of the tiger crouching in the grass.

The RAS stays in "observe, filter, and solve problems" mode so that you can enjoy life without worrying about every little thing. But how does the RAS play into marketing?

The RAS is programmed to look for patterns to make its life (and yours) easier. If you can manage to catch the attention of your prospective client's RAS by presenting a real problem, the RAS will then become activated to look for solutions to that problem.

For example, thanks to the amazing capacity of Facebook ad tracking, if I were to type in a search for the "best cat litter," I would see ads for the next few days for different kitty litter brands.

Why? My RAS is actively searching for a solution to my problem—a stinky cat box—and the company that has the most compelling ad that will solve my problem will likely get my click.

In terms of organic marketing, since you're not hyper-targeting one problem, you have to cast a slightly wider net.

Each person is struggling with multiple problems on any given day. The trouble is, most people may not know how to explain that problem. Or they may not realize there is a solution to that problem, thinking it's just something they have to suffer through.

These people have been either actively or subconsciously looking for a solution to one of their 10,000 problems for a while now (maybe even years)—and seeing your post, you speaking their problem into life, using the words they wish they knew to use, and then offering the solution—well, that's all they needed to hear.

If your solution works for them, this allows them to check off or close one box so their RAS can go on looking for solutions to other problems.

But people are fickle and easily distracted. I recently read that the average human attention span is 8.25 seconds—less than that of a goldfish.

So, Suzie or Tom may get distracted and not book you on Tuesday. But you've hooked them so well with your post that you've gotten the attention of the RAS. Suzie may decide that, for now, she doesn't have the budget to book your business or can't change service providers right now. But you're there; your business name is tucked away in her RAS on recall alert.

If you can continue to stack the right content and stay top-of-mind with Suzie and the rest of your audience with engaging content, you'll hit that lovely plane of marketing existence where reach, impressions, and touchpoints converge.

The RAS will continue to look for a solution to Suzie's problem —finding a real estate photographer that can deliver what she needs on time—and though your prices might be higher, she'll keep seeing your content through implementing my strategy.

Now that you've gotten past the first gatekeeper and aroused the RAS enough to get some engagement on a post or a click to your website, you're in. The RAS, if it thinks your solution is viable, will put your name in the "top three," so to speak, as it continues to look for a solution to Suzie's problem during this "consideration" phase of the customer journey.

In *Social Media on Auto*, you will learn how to use targeting and hashtags to get in front of the right people, tricks for writing good copy, and how to hook your potential client's RAS by using content that showcases solutions your business solves while keeping frequency high to ensure the sale.

You'll use content to mitigate and dwindle down her objections until she realizes that, expensive or not, she sees the value in your offer and your willingness to be her needed champion. Now, Suzie is willing to give you a shot.

The social media strategies taught in this book will allow your business to become top-of-mind in your customer's RAS and will help differentiate and validate your offers amidst your competition.

Touchpoints

Touchpoints represent a point of interaction between you and your customer at any point of their customer journey.

Common touchpoints include visiting a website, reading an email, replying to an email, commenting on or engaging with a social media post, reading a piece of mail, and having a phone conversation.

Touchpoints can be negative or positive.

An example of a positive touchpoint may be sending a card to your customers on their birthdays or calling mid-week to see how they are doing.

However, if your company requires several phone calls and back-and-forth emails to book your services, while those are touchpoints, they negatively affect the customer who wants to book quickly.

The key to optimizing touchpoints for an engaging, high-converting customer journey in an information-saturated world is to have the minimum number of touches necessary to convey information to make the process easier for the customer at every turn while maintaining a high customer satisfaction rating to encourage referrals.

Recency

Recency is how recently the prospect engaged with your content, your brand, or your business.

Someone who has been to your website or engaged with your social media posts in the last seven days is more likely to become a customer than someone who last engaged with your content a year ago.

Engagement Score

In social media, a metric is used to qualify the "likability" of your social media posts. This may vary a bit per platform, but for Instagram, your engagement score is calculated by taking the total number of likes, comments, shares, and views and dividing it by your total number of followers.

If your post had fifteen comments and five shares and you had 500 followers, your engagement score for that post would be calculated as follows:

$$15 + 5 = 20$$
$$20/500 = 0.04 \times 100 = 4\% \text{ Engagement Score}$$

Higher engagement scores tell the algorithm that the audience likes your content. As such, the platforms will show your content more to your followers and to new audiences, increasing your reach.

The Law of Diminishing Returns

The law of diminishing returns simply states that the same or similar actions, repeated consistently (where production remains constant), will at some point deliver less desirable results.

Using ads as an example, you could pay $200 per day for an ad campaign targeted at a small group of highly targeted people. In the first day or two, depending on the size of the audience, you may do great, generating leads for your business. By day three, however, your cost to get a lead might go from $3 per lead to $7 per lead, which makes your ad funnel unprofitable. Why?

A lot of factors are at play here, but the law of diminishing returns can be applied. Essentially, people got tired of seeing your ad and stopped clicking on it.

In social media, this correlates to posting frequency and content diversity. Basically, your content has to be balanced. You need engaging posts that are shared at just the right frequency to stay top of mind without becoming dull. If the social media algorithms see your content as non-engaging or low-engaging, they'll just quit showing it to your audience.

But don't worry; my solution neutralizes this problem and shows you how to balance it all in less than two hours a month.

Marketing Channels

Marketing channels are simply the ways we identify where to market your business.

For online marketing, when the goal is getting people to your website, the three main marketing channels are paid, organic, and affiliate.

The paid channel can then be broken down into paid search and display ads and paid social ads.

The organic channel can then be broken down into organic search, organic social, and organic direct.

The affiliate or business development channel assists in creating partnerships or affiliate offers for revenue outside of paid and organic channels.

Email marketing is also an online marketing channel. Email marketing serves as more of a conversion channel—getting people who have already visited your website and signed up for your email list to do business with you, purchase from you, attend a webinar, book a call with you, etc.

There are even more channels in print marketing, event marketing, direct mail, and more, but as this book focuses on online social media marketing in the online marketing space, I'll stop here.

CTA

CTA stands for "Call to Action". Common CTAs used in social media include "book a call," "message me to learn more," "click the link in the bio," and even fun CTAs like "drop me a :) if you think this is crazy, too!"

CTAs serve a variety of purposes, from increasing engagement on a post—so that your next two to three posts get more reach for free—to getting people to visit your website.

📷 FOCUS POINTS

In this chapter, we covered a bit of my background and introduced a glossary of common marketing terms. These terms may be used more throughout the book, so feel free to flip back to this chapter, if you have questions.

- Glossary of Terms

ACKNOWLEDGMENTS

First and foremost, thank you to my amazing team. John and Gab, I adore your creativity and attention to detail. Thank you for handling our accounts so well that you allowed me the time and brainpower needed to write this book. I love watching your families grow and hearing about your adventures. You're more than team members—you're part of our family.

I would like to thank a special group of people at Self Publishing School for pushing me to write a book. To Ashton Scriven, Leo Oliveria, Bella Rose Pope, Omer Redden, Pedro Mattos, Ida Sveningsson, Luke Worlock, Vitoria Seghetto, and Kerk Murray—thank you for encouraging me. Those 5 a.m. writing sessions were rough, but they did the trick.

I would like to thank Mike Shreeve and the Peaceful Profits team. You helped me get started and gave me the direction I needed to start and run a successful, peaceful business, as well as helped me pull this book across the finish line. Thank you.

To my friends Deb Law and Jessica Berlin, who saw the first edition of my original strategy board and said, "Oh my gosh, make a business out of this," thank you for planting the seed. To Andrea Schmidt, David Garfinkel, and so many others, thank you for speaking life into me and for believing in me so many years ago.

To my amazing clients, you've grown to be more than that; I consider you friends. Thank you for letting my team and I serve you and your families. Thank you for your friendship and support as I wrote this book.

Mie Potter, my coach and mentor, thank you for keeping me in check. Your coaching has helped me to rediscover my creativity, reduce my stress, align myself more with my own values, and strive to balance being a wife, a mother, a business owner, a homeschool mom, an author, and a friend. You helped me restore balance, and I thank you.

Thank you to my mom, dad, in-laws, and siblings. Every time I saw you, you asked me when my book would be done and held me accountable. Though this project took longer than originally planned, you encouraged me to press on. Thank God! It's done!

Finally, I would like to thank my editor, Jaclyn Reuter of River Valley Publishing. My goodness, you were thorough with your edits! I laughed so hard when I saw the first batch come through—twelve pages with audio notes! I appreciate it so much more than you know. Thank you for all your help and professionalism on this journey with me.

ABOUT THE AUTHOR

Delicia currently resides in South Carolina with her real estate photographer husband and two daughters. She has over thirteen years of online marketing experience, from working with mom-and-pop businesses to Fortune 500 companies. She loves coaching and teaching others marketing techniques to help them grow their businesses, as well as analyzing data and finding opportunities.

LOVE THIS BOOK?

Don't forget to leave a review!

Every review matters, and it matters a *lot!*

Head over to Amazon or wherever you purchased this book to leave an honest review.

Your review will help other readers, just like you, find the solution they need to save themselves time and frustration with their business's social media strategy.

Thanks so much!
Delicia Ivins

Made in the USA
Columbia, SC
09 January 2024